The Lady Killer

Kristen Morden

Published by Trellis Publishing, 2021.

While every precaution has been taken in the preparation of this book, the publisher assumes no responsibility for errors or omissions, or for damages resulting from the use of the information contained herein.

THE LADY KILLER

First edition. June 28, 2021.

ISBN: 979-8223018537

Written by Kristen Morden.

THE LADY KILLER

KIRSTEN MORDEN

1

Ricardo Silvio Caputo was born in Mendoza, Argentina in 1949. As a child, he was very athletic with a love of running and swimming, and became skilled in martial arts. He taught himself to become an accomplished sketch artist and became fluent in various languages. He grew into a very handsome young man. His dark hair, dimpled chin, and deep eyes, accompanied with his charming personality, drew people to him. He enjoyed the attention he received from women and tended to seek out intelligent partners who he could hold a conversation with, and preferred women who would sympathize with his frustrations in life. It wasn't difficult to be won over by Ricardo's smooth, winning personality. In 1970, at the age of twenty-one, Ricardo travelled to the United States on a six-month visa. He held a number of jobs, from a busboy and waiter in various restaurants, to a custodian in the Plaza Hotel, and eventually decided to stay in the country for an extended period. This attractive and ambitious young man would become a regular on the FBI's most wanted list over the course of the 1970s, often holding the number one spot. Behind the sombre eyes hid a dangerous mix of personalities with a terrifying aggression towards women.

Long Island's Roslyn High School 1969 yearbook described Natalie Brown as a bright and adventurous student with a love of horse riding and swimming. Growing up in her family home in Long Island, she held ambitions of following in her mother's footsteps to become a nurse. In 1970, aged eighteen, Natalie decided to take a break from her studies. She got a job as a teller at Marine Midland Bank, working in the midtown-Manhattan branch. Her branch was situated just a few blocks away from the Plaza Hotel where twenty-one-year-old Ricardo Caputo was working. He would cash his checks at the midtown-Manhattan Marine Midland Bank, which is where he first met Natalie. Striking up small talk, as was his nature, Natalie and Ricardo became familiar over the following weeks, with Natalie eventually asking if he would like to meet her in a less formal environment. Ricardo leapt at the chance and offered to take her out that very evening. The pair began a year-long relationship that would end in tragedy.

Natalie's parents disapproved of this budding romance, concerned it was moving too quickly. Just three months into their relationship, Natalie and Ricardo left for a vacation in the Caribbean, enjoying the freedom offered to them, swimming in the sea and staying in hostels or sleeping under palm trees on public beaches. As their vacation drew to a close, Ricardo suggested they didn't return home, venturing instead to explore Florida and California. Natalie agreed, and the pair made their way through Miami to Los Angeles, eventually arriving in San Francisco. After several weeks of funding their trip, homebody Natalie wanted to return to the Brown's home in Flower Hill, New York. Strapped for cash, Ricardo agreed to accompany her, and they began hitch-hiking their way back to the North-East. When they returned, Mr and Mrs Brown were shocked to discover the young couple were engaged to be married, perhaps in an effort to combat Ricardo's now expired visa. But Natalie began to change her mind about the idea soon after their return to New York, and started to consider leaving Ricardo.

At 7.30pm on July 31, 1971, Natalie and Ricardo were left alone in the Brown family home as Natalie's parents went out to dinner. At 8.30pm, the Sixth Precinct received a phone call from a man who stated, "I think I killed my girlfriend." Officers arrived at the house on Flower Hill soon after to find nineteen-year-old Natalie Brown had been violently stabbed to death in the kitchen. Ricardo confessed to the crime on the spot, hinting at the nature of the argument. Officers believed he was indicating the couple had argued about Natalie's intention to end the relationship. He was immediately arrested and awaited his trial. Authorities swiftly began their investigation into Ricardo's history, learning that he had arrived in America from Argentina with no criminal record or official history of psychiatric problems. However, they did discover that Ricardo had been treated for mental illness during his teenage years. Concerns were raised further as officers reported Ricardo for "talking with the deceased" in his jail cell, believing himself to be haunted. Testing his mental state, psychiatrists found him unable to stand trial. Acquitted by reason of insanity, Ricardo Caputo was consequently sent to Matteawan State Hospital for the Criminally Insane.

It was during his time as an inmate in Matteawan that Ricardo met Judith Becker. In her mid-twenties, Judith was a highly intelligent woman from Long Island who easily made friends. She had graduated from Connecticut State College before advancing on to St John's University at Queens, New York, where she gained a Master's degree in psychology and had a dream of working with disadvantaged children. After graduating, she was offered a position as a staff psychologist at Matteawan. Although a step away from her ambition of working with children, she accepted, believing she could help anyone. She was very dedicated to her job and didn't hold much of a social life outside of her working hours. A few boyfriends came and went, but she remained a reserved woman focused on advancing her career. Ricardo became one of Judith's patients at Matteawan, and the pair quickly developed a close friendship. Whether or not the pair were dating has been hotly debated by investigators, researchers, and family, with Judith's parents remaining adamant their relationship was purely platonic.

As Ricardo's sentence continued, he was considered an exemplary patient. He caused no trouble and was deemed to be of no harm to himself or others. In October 1973, he was transferred to Manhattan Psychiatric Centre on Wards Island, a minimum-security asylum where he worked at the hospital snack bar for minimum wage and was granted regular furloughs. During these days of leave from the institution, Ricardo would make his way to Judith's apartment in Yonkers. Judith's mother, Jane Becker, later recalled, "Every chance he was allowed out, a few times a week, he would come to her apartment. She tried to befriend him." The pair began to spend more and more time together outside of hospital settings. In the summer of 1974, Judith invited Ricardo to her parents' home to spend the day by the pool in their backyard. Unaware that he was a criminal patient, her parents welcomed him into their home. As Jane Becker remembers, "He was very charming. He seemed very intelligent, quite personable."

Ricardo continued to come and go from the Manhattan Psychiatric Centre. Such a trusted patient, his movements were unquestioned, which would prove troubling in October 1974 with staff only realizing he was missing days after he had officially broken out and disappeared. Cracks in their relationship – whether professional, friendly, or romantic – began to show in September of 1974 when Judith asked Ricardo to stop coming to her apartment. He continued to do so regardless of her wishes, becoming all the more persistent. On October 21, 1974, Judith's parents arrived at her apartment in Yonkers, concerned that they hadn't heard from their reliable daughter for hours. Letting themselves into her apartment, they began to look around. They found twenty-six-year-old Judith dead in her bedroom, badly beaten and strangled with one of her nylon stockings. Mrs Becker would later claim, "When I realized she had been murdered, I knew it was him." When police arrived on the scene, they discovered that Judith had also been robbed. Ricardo had taken her money and her 1972 Plymouth Duster, and fled the area.

Ricardo made his way across the United States, eventually arriving in San Francisco. He adopted a new identity upon his arrival, going by the name of Ricardo Dunoguier, pretending to be a struggling artist from Uruguay. He openly boasted about his fluent knowledge of Spanish, English, Portuguese, Hebrew, and Italian, and put his childhood love of sketching to good use, drawing faces in bars to earn a meagre living. He was only in San Francisco for a few months, but it was long enough to meet twenty-eight-year-old Barbara Ann Taylor and begin a whirlwind romance with her. Meeting Barbara in a pub, he offered to sketch her. She agreed, and ultimately bought the drawing from this mysterious stranger. Soon after, they were dating. Ricardo quickly moved into her Pacific Heights apartment, and she bought him expensive meals, fine clothes, and impressive hiking boots which he wore on a hiking vacation to Yosemite park. But Barbara soon grew tired of providing for Ricardo with little in return.

In early March, 1975, Barbara began to indicate her displeasure with the couple's situation. Police Inspector Earl Sanders would later state, "He was pretty much sponging off her, that was his game. She was happy at first. He was a very charming man. But her family and friends were skeptical because he didn't have a job and he talked big." In an attempt to get some space, Barbara purchased Ricardo a ticket to fly to Honolulu. He had previously expressed interest in moving there to find restaurant work, and she hoped the trip would encourage him to find a career whilst buying her time to consider her next move, ultimately hoping he might not return. Ricardo left for two weeks, and returned on March 26. Barbara met him at the airport and drove to her apartment. When they arrived at Pacific Heights, Ricardo spoke of marriage. Barbara would later tell her sister that she desperately wanted to break off the relationship. On the morning of March 27, a neighbour saw Ricardo leaving Barbara's apartment with a suitcase. Just a few days later, Barbara's family grew concerned when she failed to show up at a family dinner at her parents' home in Fremont, San Francisco Bay, on March 30. They urgently called the police, who later arrived at her apartment to find her beaten to death. Ricardo's fingerprints were found at the crime scene, but by the time Barbara's body was discovered, the culprit was long gone, once again fleeing the area. Police circulated photographs of the so-called Ricardo Dunoguier, and many immediately spotted the resemblance to New York killer, Ricardo Caputo.

Ricardo, now adopting the surname Diaz, was running toward Mexico. He neared the border just five days after Barbara was found in her apartment. However, his attempts to cross the border to Mexico were foiled as immigration officials detained him in El Paso, Texas on April 3. To these officials, he gave the name Ricardo Pinto. He was held in a detention centre for just four days, managing to escape confinement on April 7. Using his charming personality once again, he befriended two other detainees. Together, they took a guard hostage, clambered over the chain-link fence that surrounded the facility, and stole a car, driving as fast as they could towards Mexico. The authorities quickly caught up with the trio, but Ricardo managed to avoid being recaptured and fled for Mexico City.

When he arrived in Mexico City, Ricardo found a sales job in a bookstore. It was here that he met Laura Gomez, a woman in her early twenties, enrolled in a graduate program in industrial psychology at the local university. The pair began dating, unknown to Laura's parents who believed they were only friends. They remained together for two years, secretly meeting for romantic encounters at Ricardo's apartment. As with his previous girlfriends, Laura was very attentive and nurturing. Coming from an affluent family, she ensured Ricardo always had what he needed – or wanted. On October 3, 1977, Laura Gomez was found dead in her apartment, having been tortured then bludgeoned to death. Her father knew immediately that her boyfriend was responsible. During her autopsy, it was discovered that Laura was two months pregnant. Ricardo Caputo, assumed to be the child's father, was once again long gone from the crime scene.

Ricardo Caputo's movements for the seventeen years that followed are relatively unclear. Investigators and reporters have pieced together a rough outline, but had to rely primarily upon the word and cooperation of an unreliable character. After the murder in Mexico City, Ricardo reportedly returned to the US in 1977, settling in the Los Angeles area for nearly six years. He found work in a local restaurant, eventually becoming the manager. It was here that he met Jasmine Fernandez. The couple married in 1979, and together they had two children. A son was born in 1981, and his daughter in 1984. Whilst

Jasmine was in labour with their second child, Ricardo took the family's money and fled once again, later claiming that he became paranoid that Jasmine had begun to notice some of his odd behaviour, such as talking with a non-existent person. He returned to South America once again, living in Guadalajara. In 1985, he met seventeen-year-old Susana Elizondo. Just months after meeting – and despite still being married to Jasmine – the couple married. Using his plethora of false IDs, he returned to the US under the alias of Franco Parose, this time finding a home in the Chicago area where he found steady work, primarily at Arlington Raceway and as a restaurant manager, and secured visas for Susana and their newborn son. The couple remained in Chicago for the next seven years, building a family together. He held various jobs, working as a salesman, a karate instructor, in restaurants, and even as an English teacher around the Midwest area. But in 1992, he returned to Argentina once again with his second family. This time, he worked as a salesman for a medical supplies company, which granted him flexible and regular travel to Miami to buy supplies, all the while crossing the border with a fake passport and false papers.

These seventeen years are considered to be Ricardo Caputo's quiet years. His lawyer, Michael Kennedy, would state, "Normally, what one sees in psycho-pathology and schizophrenia is that the anti-social behavior increases in frequency and magnitude over time, and one just doesn't stop. In this instance, it stopped. Yet he lives – having committed four horrible murders – a totally quiescent life, with a wife and four wonderful children." Yet, Ricardo's reasoning for moving around so frequently has never been entirely clear. Some speculate his final return to Argentina was spurred on by the airing of an episode dedicated to his past crimes on "America's Most Wanted" in 1991. Others believe he fled the area to avoid being caught for the murders of two women, becoming a prime suspect in both cases. Twenty-three-year-old Devon Green worked with Ricardo in a restaurant in Los Angeles. In 1981, four years after Ricardo Caputo claimed he had changed his ways, Devon's body was found, brutally murdered. Another co-worker was aware of a blossoming friendship between Devon and Ricardo in the days before her death, though he has never been conclusively linked to the crime. Two years later on August 2, 1983, sixty-three-year-old Jacqueline Bernard was found dead, having been strangled in her Riverside Drive apartment in Manhattan, New York. Jacqueline was a well-liked and much-admired social activist who had befriended Ricardo. A man who appeared to resemble Ricardo was caught by Jacqueline's landlord attempting to break into her apartment. Both of these murders remain unsolved, but friends and relatives believe Ricardo Caputo is guilty. On January 22, 1985, a private investigator researching Jacqueline's death at her family's request received an anonymous tip, with a caller claiming Ricardo was the killer. The unknown source claimed he had overheard the Argentinian man bragging about murdering several other women, and even a few men. One of Jacqueline's closest friends, Linda Wolfe, even went so far as to conduct her own research, desperate to find evidence to implicate Ricardo to finally get justice for her friend. This led to Wolfe writing the memoir, "Love Me To Death", which recounted Ricardo Caputo's movements.

In February 1994, Ricardo Caputo arrived at his mother's house in Argentina. He had not seen or contacted his family for over twenty years. He was prepared to hand himself in. His mother contacted Ricardo's brother, Alberto, who in turn hired a lawyer, Michael Kennedy, who would stay by Ricardo's side for the duration of his prosecution. Ricardo alleged that he had been vividly haunted by memories of his crimes over the course of a year, and claimed he was concerned that his dark side would return to him. He stated multiple personalities would take over his body and mind, leaving him out of control. In a press release shortly after his arrest, Mr Kennedy stated his client's memory "was in bits and pieces, and he couldn't say when, if ever, this psychotic personality would re-emerge." Ricardo openly confessed to the murders of Natalie Brown, Judith Becker, Barbara Ann Taylor, and Laura Gomez, unafraid of facing punishment. Upon handing himself in to the authorities, he stated, "I would rather have my body locked up and my mind free, than living as I was, with another identity, with my mind locked up and my body free." Flummoxed by the case, Mr Kennedy claimed he believed Ricardo Caputo to be a schizophrenic and psychotic, but this brought considerable scepticism from mental health professionals, as schizophrenia tends to involve delusions and hallucinations, not multiple personalities. Consequently, Ricardo was required to undergo mental health testing to ensure he was indeed sane and capable of standing trial, being held in Nassau County Jail without bail until a conclusion had been reached.

Doctor Fernando Linares was charged with testing Ricardo's mental capabilities, and his findings were later made public. It didn't take long for Ricardo to introduce the doctor to three other personalities which he claimed lived within him. The first was Frank, a working man who put food on the table and was sensible with money. The second was Robert, who was strong, healthy, and charismatic, and longed for a stable family life. The third was Richard, who he described as "weak and sick, like a kid playing with a ball, playing in the street." The doctor noted that there would often be disagreements between the personalities known as Frank and Robert. However, Doctor Linares did not rule out the possibility of Ricardo being "a psychopathic personality pretending to be crazy."

Ricardo stated that his violent behaviour was triggered whenever he felt trapped in a relationship. When discussing the murder of Judith Becker, he claimed "She began to require a lot of sex from me, and that is when I began to change." However, this contradicts his possessive behaviour displayed within his relationships with his victims. His memories of the events also proved unreliable. Doctor Linares believed he possibly suffered from periods of intense psychosis, losing the perception of reality, as well as his sanity. Ricardo stated that he would often hear loud, shouting voices, and his vision would be blurred with countless wide lines. When discussing the murders of both Natalie Brown and Judith Becker, Ricardo claimed he could only remember the voices and lines. Upon fleeing to Mexico City, he felt depressed and could hear the voices more frequently, stating that he was hearing them almost constantly, declaring they "did not let me have any peace," and that he eventually became desperate. He admitted that he could not remember escaping from the immigration detention centre and crossing the border, describing his return to South America as an out of body experience "I thought I was a ghost." Doctor Linares was baffled by the case, unsure about Roberto's sincerity. However, he later stated, "It is a strange case. From the moment he arrived ... He always had the same expression on his face. It did not change at all. It was one of guilt. He said he intended to repay the damage. And as the days went by he was even more desperate and anxious to give up. He is definitely a very very sick man."

Doctor Linares investigated Ricardo's childhood in an effort to uncover the root of his potential psychiatric problems. What he discovered were tales of physical abuse. Ricardo accused his mother of abandoning their family until his father passed away, returning with a partner who regularly slapped him, calling the man a "tyrant". He also claimed that he was raped at the age of seven or eight by a stranger in Mendoza who had enticed him with the offer of candy. At the age of eighteen, Ricardo voluntarily signed into a psychiatric hospital suffering from depression where he told the doctors about his experience of rape and abuse. Mr Kennedy was certain this abuse he received as a child contributed heavily towards his schizophrenia. However, some remain dubious about these claims. Alberto admitted their childhood home was not the most stable, but found it hard to believe it would cause a psychotic break in his brother. Mr Kennedy was also criticised for leaning heavily on his client's potential mental health issues for his own gain in the case, not allowing the media to contact Ricardo for comments, and displaying frustration at extensive police questioning without his presence. Should the case go to trial, Kennedy would be forced to rely on insanity as his defence, and prove that Ricardo was incapable of recognising the nature of his actions or knowing he was wrong at the time he committed the murders, so acquittal by reason of insanity would work in Kennedy's favour.

Looking at all of the evidence and Doctor Linares' findings, John Dunne, the Nassau County judge assigned to the case, decided to reverse the decision made in court twenty-three years previously. Describing Ricardo Caputo as "a brutal and cunning man," he found him to be fit for trial. On January 31, 1995, Caputo pleaded guilty to manslaughter in the Natalie Brown murder case, claiming "I stabbed Natalie to death, and I was very emotionally disturbed at the time." Judge John Dunne was unsympathetic to Ricardo's statement, responding "Having led a life of murder, mayhem and manipulation for the past twenty-five years, it is obviously your belief that a few words of sympathy and mea culpa will make you a free man." On April 6, 1995, Dunne sentenced him to twenty-five years in prison for Natalie's murder. Ricardo returned to court on June 29, 1995, for the murder of Judith Becker. Once again, he pleaded guilty, and was sentenced with twenty-five years to life. He was never sentenced for the murders of Barbara Ann Taylor and Laura Gomez. In October 1997, playing in the prison courtyard during recreational time while awaiting his next trial, Ricardo Caputo, "The Lady Killer," died of a fatal heart attack, aged forty-eight. The man who had terrorised women across two countries, and who was reportedly terrified of his own psyche, was gone.

Ricardo Caputo was a dangerous man who adopted at least seventeen aliases over the course of twenty years. With his devilish charm and attractive looks, he was able to draw a huge number of women into his life, ending in catastrophe. Possessive and determined, he brought heart-break to two families in New York when he coldly murdered both Natalie Brown and Judith Becker who had each attempted to leave him, rejecting his marriage proposals. He seduced and manipulated people wherever he went, leeching off of wealthy Barbara Ann Taylor in San Francisco and Laura Gomez in Mexico City before brutally killing them both and Gomez's unborn child. Whether he is truly guilty of murdering Devon Green and Jacqueline Bernard is uncertain, but he remains a primary suspect in both cases. Ricardo was a truly bewildering man who puzzled lawyers, psychiatrists, and the general public alike. Whether he was truly mentally ill or whether he was a master manipulator will also remain unsolved. However, his eventual detainment provided some closure for grieving families who had lost beloved daughters, sisters, and friends. Upon his arrest, Judith Becker's mother, aged seventy-four, stated, "I'm relieved. I always felt he might be murdering other people. It has been very emotional, very draining."

COLD BLOODED CHARMER : SERIAL KILLER SHAWN GRATE

14

JESSE DIXON

A desperate plea for help

On September 13, 2016, a call came through Ashland, Ohio's 911 system from a distressed woman, who claimed to be held captive in a home.

"I've been abducted," she whispered to the dispatcher. "Please hurry."

The police who arrived at the scene not only rescued the woman who had placed the call, but also discovered two dead bodies – left there by Shawn Michael Grate, a 40-year-old man who had a reputation for being a "cold-blooded charmer." Grate also brought police to a third body, located in a wooded area by a ravine in neighbouring Richland County. And, as the investigation continued, police uncovered connections to two more murders.

"(He is) obviously a serial killer," said Marion County Sheriff Tim Bailey. "It's hard to believe others aren't out there."

The cold-blooded charmer

"He was charming. He was always smiling, and he had those big blue eyes," said Amy Smith, remembering Grate as a teenager in Marion, Ohio. "All the girls liked Shawn."

As irresistible as he was, multiple women recall experiencing Grate's dark side early on. By the age of 18, Grate had revealed himself to be jealous, controlling, and violent – and was even arrested for grabbing the throat of his young girlfriend.

When he was only 23, Grate broke into the home his pregnant 17-year-old girlfriend, where he choked her and, according to Marion police reports, threatened to kill her. And only eight months later, he hid all night under the girl's couch before assaulting her and her sister with a butcher knife.

"(Grate) told them to shut up because he was in control," reported an officer at the scene. "Then he said if anyone comes to the door, there will not be anyone here to answer it, so you better hope that no one knocks at the door."

In addition to this pregnancy, Grate is known to have fathered at least two other children. Two were with girlfriends in Marion, and the third is the product of a brief marriage in Mansfield. According to court documents, Grate's ex-wife said he once threatened that "if I can't see my daughter, then no one will."

Grate's criminal history is fairly extensive – but until 2016, he'd only spent about four years in prison for a burglary in Marion, violating early release conditions with an assault, and for domestic violence. Grate had also been charged several times with offences relating to drugs and alcohol.

Grate grew up in Marion County, the product of a broken home. His mother, Teresa McFarland, left his father, Terry Grate, in 1982 – and eventually relinquished custody of both Grate and his older brother, Ronald, to her ex-husband.

McFarland still resides in rural Ashland County, and has discussed her son in only one interview to date. She told the Daily Mail, a British tabloid, that her son changed after getting involved with drugs and spending time in prison – and added that for the past three years, Grate had been estranged from the rest of the family.

"Yes, he's good looking, but the devil's good looking, too," McFarland said. "He ain't got no red horns and all that stuff. You find out he's charming, and of course, that charm can charm the pants off anybody."

It's this charm that Grate uses to get what he wants. He's been described as lazy by many people who have recently come in contact with him – and rather than work, people say he prefers to take advantage of kind, vulnerable people, particularly women with money.

Wally Toward, a businessman in Mansfield who owns several properties, saw Grate attempt to move in with several of his female tenants.

"Grate always mistook kindness for weakness," Toward said. "He exploited kind people."

By his late 20s, Grate was beginning to show signs of mental health issues. According to Smith, Grate's teenage friend, he would frequently invest all his energy into a project before completely giving up on it after only a couple of weeks.

"He would just give up on everything," she said.

His erratic behaviour was a concern to a female friend of Smith's, who had dated Grate around 1999 but eventually broke up with him because he "wasn't acting right."

"He would get very, very depressed," Smith said. "My girlfriend would say, '(he) is not wanting to get off the couch. It's been days.'"

In 2005, Grate started dating another young woman named Christina Hildreth. The couple dated for about five years, and eventually lived together in Crawford County.

"He was very handsome and quite charming," she recalled. "He had a way of looking at you like you were the only person he saw."

However, after they moved into the same residence, Grate began to reveal his controlling, jealous tendencies – and it was hard for Hildreth to deal with.

"He started showing a side of himself that was cold and indifferent," she admitted. "He wanted me to himself."

It wasn't just his relationships with women that escalated, however. Tim Denis, who used to be a close friend of Grate's, said the friendship fell apart over a bad loan. When Denis refused to provide Grate with financial support, he received a string of angry text messages from his friend – and admitted the last message "still gives him chills.

"Meet the other me," Grate had messaged.

A growing threat

Following the divorce of his parents, Grate lived with his mother in Marion County, where he completed high school in 1995. At that time, he was a close friend of Smith's, who said she remembers him as her "go-to person" and a "shoulder to cry on."

"He was the one that came to a Halloween party dressed as a woman, making everyone laugh and has nothing but a smile on his face," she recalled. "That is the Shawn I know. That is the Shawn I want to remember."

Grate was the literal boy next door for Julia Pennington-Smith, who graduated from River Valley in 1995. She remembers Grate as one of her childhood best friends – not as a serial killer.

"I knew him from the time I was five years old," she said. "We grew up together. We were neighbours. We went to school together. We used to play backyard football, we used to play softball. They were like my brothers; I loved the family."

While Pennington-Smith said she hadn't been in contact with Grate since they graduated from high school, the two were friends on Facebook.

"I don't remember him being troubled," she said. "I don't remember him ever getting into any trouble. He lived a normal life."

But Grate's first adult arrest happened just weeks after he turned 18, while he was still in high school. While his juvenile record is unknown, there are police reports available detailing his early run-ins with the law.

The first arrest was the result of a domestic incident, after his girlfriend at the time claimed she had been trying to end the relationship for the past six months. However, the couple was still together and had a new baby when she reported a second domestic incident in January 1996.

"He seems to be involved in nonviolent crime except when dealing with females, especially those he is intimate with," said Tristin Kilgallon, who teaches a class on serial killers at Ohio Northern University, where he works as an assistant professor of criminal justice.

Later that same year, Grate was convicted of a felony charge after committing a burglary with a juvenile, and was sentenced to four years in prison. He served only seven months and was released early – but his violence continued to escalate.

In 1999, when he was 22, Grate's 17-year-old girlfriend told police that he had choked her nearly unconscious – while she was two months pregnant with his child.

"(His girlfriends) are getting younger... why? Are they easier to manipulate?" Kilgallon inquired. "He chokes her – this is up close and personal."

Still, the incident resulted in less than a month's worth of jailtime for Grate. Although the teenage girl's family pursued a restraining order against Grate, the young woman had the no-contact order removed just a few months later.

Even after Grate's second child was born, the relationship continued to struggle. His son was born in September, and only a month later, Grate threatened his son's mother and her sister with the butcher knife. During the struggle over the knife, both Grate and the young girl sustained minor to severe cuts.

"He steps it up," said Kilgallon. "He's using a weapon now."

This incident meant a longer period of incarceration for Grate, as his early release was revoked in 2000 and he was forced to serve what was left of his original four-year sentence. The prosecutor on the case said a separate prison term was initially sought for the new conviction, but the judge sentenced Grate to probation only.

In January 2003, Grate was released from prison again – and by October, he was already in more trouble with the law. Another domestic charge came as a result of a complaint received from the mother of Grate's second child, stating that he had choked her and forced her to perform a sex act on him. No sexual assault charges were laid, but Grate was charged with two counts of misdemeanor domestic violence – and went back to prison until May 2004.

Grate mostly laid low for the next couple years, with records showing nothing but minor run-ins with the law – but Grate has admitted now that his first kill was in 2005, an unidentified woman who was distributing newspapers and magazines in his neighbourhood.

In 2005, Grate started dating Hildreth, who he moved in with a year later. He was upset that her children were living with them as well, Hildreth said, but said he was primarily just mentally abusive – although she does recall some physical violence, as well.

The worst incident happened in June 2010, Hildreth said, when Grate assaulted her repeatedly – with multiple blows to her face, and grabbing her roughly by the throat. She even fractured her hand in an attempt to defend herself from the falling blows.

Grate did eventually bring Hildreth to the emergency room, and they told the hospital staff that she'd fallen. However, as soon as she was left alone with a nurse, Hildreth explained what had actually happened. While police were informed immediately, Grate managed to escape arrest temporarily – but was arrested four days later, when Hildreth told the authorities that she was concerned Grate was hiding inside her couch.

Grate was charged with a first-degree misdemeanor domestic violence, and received a sentence of 180 days in jail. Despite the issuing of a protection order, Grate continued to call Hildreth from jail, and sent letters that he addressed to her cats. Hildreth, however, ended their relationship after incident, and to this day, believes it kept both her and her children alive.

"Before that night, I feared he would kill me," she recalled. "That night only strengthened that fear. I now believe more than ever had I not left him, I would be dead or one of my children would be."

The family man

Grate settled down with a new partner in 2011, a 28-year-old Mansfield woman named Amber Nicole Bowman. The couple were married and living together in the ranch house she owned when she gave birth to their daughter in July 2012.

Despite her young marriage and a brand new baby, though, Bowman filed for divorce in October 2012, citing "serious and unfortunate differences" in the separation agreement filed in December of that year.

Bowman sought a restraining order just a few months later, in April 2013 – claiming Grate had been calling her at work and making threats that if he couldn't see his daughter, "no one else will." He demanded money from Bowman, to "help him get back on his feet." He was also not paying child support for any of the three children he had fathered so far.

That June, the Richland County Child Support Enforcement Agency informed the county's domestic relations court that they had reason to believe that Grate was unemployed, and by September, a contempt of court order was issued against him for failure to seek work. He'd apparently been moving from place to place in Mansfield, but was technically homeless.

"He was not mentally disabled, he was not physically disabled," Toward said, who frequently worried Grate would steal rent money from his female tenants. "He could hold a job if he chose to, but instead of that he always chose to maneuver people to con them into helping him."

During this time frame, Grate was getting to know two women – Rebekah Leicy and Candice Cunningham. Leicy was a prostitute who worked in the Third Street area, the same area where Grate's ex-girlfriend Amber White used to work.

"He picked me up, I used to prostitute," White recalled, adding that he would only have about $10 or $20 to spend on sexual favours. "He was shy. He didn't talk (during sex), and he wanted the lights off. I was mean to him because I was strung out on drugs and he just disappeared."

Originally, Leicy's death was ruled as a drug overdose when her body was discovered in March 2015, in a wooded area of Ashland

County. After speaking with Grate following his arrest in September 2016, however, police have reopened the case and are investigating the possibility that Grate may be responsible for her death.

Cunningham and Grate were living together in Mansfield when she went missing in June 2015. When he was arrested, Grate informed police that they could find the body of a woman near a burned out house in nearby Madison Township. The body has yet to be identified, but evidence indicates it is likely Cunningham.

Foiled

Grate claims he wanted to marry the woman who called 911 on September 13 – a call that led to her rescue, and his arrest. The abduction victim, who has yet to be identified, occasionally played badminton with Grate at her apartment complex in Ashland – until she was kidnapped and forced to endured two days of involuntary sexual activity before she was able to place a call to police.

The chilling 19-minute call reveals a terrified woman whispering to a dispatcher in a quavering voice – identifying Grate by name, describing a nearby laundromat, informing police that Grate was armed with a taser, and reassuring the dispatcher that she was not bleeding, "anymore."

"I'm in the bedroom with him," she said, her voice hushed. "I'm scared."

The abducted woman lived in the same area as one of the other women whose body police discovered at the home, 29-year-old Elizabeth Griffith. According to Griffith's friends, she and Grate had dated, and Griffith had been missing since August 16.

"The short time I talked to her she cried several times, just about life and how she couldn't find anyone to love her," Grate said in a rare interview from jail in October 2016. "She had a mental illness."

Police discovered her body stuffed in an upstairs closet in the vacant home, and another body in the basement – Stacey Stanley, a

43-year-old woman from Greenwich who had been reported missing only days earlier.

According to Stanley's son, Kurtis, she hadn't come home after going out for a coffee and stopping at a gas station with a flat tire. Grate said he "helped" the woman before taking her back to the home where he had been squatting.

"It is a sad situation, especially the way she died," said Stanley's uncle, Argil Stanley. "She was beaten to death. The cops said she was unrecognizable from the beating."

After police uncovered the two bodies inside the house, Grate admitted to killing another woman in Richland County, and proceeded to bring police to her body – the body believed to be Candice Cunningham. He confessed that he'd also killed Leicy and another woman whose name he couldn't remember, back in 2005. His first kill, he said.

While the abduction victim who called 911 has not been identified publicly, her family has spoken out about the incident – and claim they will never forgive Grate for what he put her through. The victim's father said the family was fully supportive of the death penalty, which Grate has admitted that he deserves.

According to the victim's brother, Grate preyed on the woman's faith to develop a relationship with her – and eventually kidnap her.

"If somebody wanted to be a predator, like this guy obviously was, he could just feed off that and sense that," said the victim's brother. "As long as she would have somebody who would listen to that, oh, he could do whatever he wanted, manipulate however he wanted. That's the way I pretty much believe it went down."

Grate did admit to police that he is religious, as were a number of his victims. He said the women were lonely, and seemed to have lost their way – even claiming that they didn't even want to go on living.

In a confession, Grate explained that he would hug his victims and remind them that "we are all in this together," before choking them.

According to Grate, he would give his victims one last opportunity to beg for their lives – and if they didn't, he would end it for them.

So far, Grate has admitted to killing five women, and claims four of them were "choked out." His first victim, however, was stabbed in the throat. Grate believes her name was Dana, but her body has not been identified yet.

According to Grate, "Dana" delivered magazines and newspapers throughout his mother's neighbourhood in Marion, Ohio – but was "scheming" his mother out of her subscription.

"I remember her trying to sell them to me," Grate recalled. "Me and my mom would be on the porch and she'd try to sell them. My mom said she wasn't getting her subscriptions delivered."

Since he had company coming over soon, he didn't have time to strangle his first victim. Instead, he stabbed her in the throat and left her in the basement. Eventually, he brought her body out to Victory Road in Marion, where it stayed until it was discovered two years later. Currently, the only information the Marion County sheriff's department has to help make an identification is a sketch.

Grate also confessed to killing Leicy ten years later, although her death had already been ruled as drug related. According to Grate, the two had met at a bar, and she'd tried to steal $4 from him while he was in the restroom – so he strangled her, like the other three more recent victims.

Cunningham was killed in a vacant house the couple was squatting in, according to Grate, and he went back and burned the house down to hide her body. Police records show that the house had been destroyed in a suspicious fire on June 21 – the day after Grate successfully fled an officer who'd stopped him on a felony child support warrant.

"We were seeing each other for about seven months," Grate said of Cunningham. "She was pretty violent and suicidal, I turned her into a psych ward for about a week. Then we fought at the house in Richland for three to four days. Then the next day we'd get up and go for walks.

She could have run off and told police at any time ... She would take handfuls of pills at a time and I would give her the water."

Police are still collecting evidence and DNA to connect Grate to all five murders. Currently, he's been indicted on 23 charges – including aggravated murder for the deaths of Stanley and Griffith and kidnapping for the abduction of the victim who escaped. Each murder count carries the possibility of a prison term of 15 years to life, and the kidnapping charge could be punishable by 3 to 11 years in prison.

Charges have not been filed on the other three murders Grate claims to be responsible for. According to Ashland County Prosecutor Chris Tunnell, a "large volume" of evidence has been collected by the state Bureau of Criminal Identification and Investigation, the Ashland Police Department, and other agencies.

"A clear vision of WHY."

About a month after his arrest, Grate sent two letters to a Cleveland reporter, acknowledging his part in the five killings – and providing what he claimed was his motive for murdering the women. The letters were a response to a request for an on-camera interview.

"That sounds scary in facing myself even more," Grate's first letter stated. "The mirror has been enough but having more questions hitting me straight on could and would only help to understand me better."

The second letter explains Grate's motive for committing a "horrible act of violent behavior," stating that while in jail, he was able to gain a "clear vision of WHY."

"They were already dead, just their bodies were flopping wherever it can flop but their minds were already dead!" Grate wrote. "The state took their minds. Once they started receiving their monthly cheques."

Grate blames "government assistance" for robbing his victims of their "minds," and said that while he applied for government assistance five years ago, all he received was a $197 food card over a year and a half.

"Many bodies received 700," he wrote – using the words "people," "victims," and "bodies" interchangeably throughout the letters.

The letters are also full of Bible verses, specifically passages from the Book of Revelation and Hebrews.

"I feel I deserve the death penalty," he said in an October 2016 interview from prison, "but I also feel I can help some people in here … I'm just trying to free myself of what I've done. I'm afraid of the death penalty … I'd like to die on my own and not by the state."

Grate's mother, McFarland, said that she feels terrible for the trauma her son inflicted on his victims – and their families.

"it feels like a nightmare," she said. "I pray for the families. It's like a death to me too, and I have to grieve."

Jekyll and Hyde

Grate has claimed he feels some remorse for the murders – "50/50," he told a reporter.

According to Kilgallon, Grate is a perfect example of a killer motivated by a need for power and control. Often, he said, these killers are intelligent and charismatic – and master manipulators. When manipulation tactics fail, however, they will turn to violence.

Kilgallon added Grate was successful in covering his tracks each time, and despite frequently physically and sexually abusing his partners, they stayed with him – sometimes even for years. While Grate may have a specific victim type, he may prey on specific women simply because he finds them "easy targets."

"What we know about men, specifically that are violent against women, is that they feel entitled to be violent or justified in their violence," said Nancy Radcliffe, HelpLine of Delaware and Morrow Counties' director of sexual assault services.

Radcliffe's experience in the area of intimate partner violence spans more than 25 years, and while she has not assessed Grate's case personally, said he may fit the "Jekyll and Hyde" model of domestic abusers.

"On the outside, on any given day, they seem to be very outstanding members of society – people that you would look up to or wouldn't be at all threatened by," she explained. "But there's this other persona that comes out from time to time, and usually towards the person that they want to see it."

Toward, who claimed he's always prided himself on his ability to read people, admitted that he "missed the boat" when it came to Grate. And while he has had confrontations with a number of people during his time delivering subpoenas for local attorneys, he doesn't like to think about the fact that he made have had some "vivid discussions" with a potential serial killer.

"When I look back and try to analyze why I could not read him was because he is truly evil," Toward said. "For every Mother Theresa, there's a Charlie Manson – and he is Mansfield's Charlie Manson. He is a sociopath. You can't read a sociopath because there's no soul to read."

SERIAL KILLING COP : THE TRUE STORY OF MIKHAIL POPKOV

FRANK COLEMAN

'He is charming and sociable. Women like him but he is a beast inside, and it is always hard to fight a werewolf.' - Mikhail Zavorin, police investigator

Mikhail Popkov may be the most prolific serial killers in world history.

He led a double-life as a family man with a wife and a young daughter. But after the dissolution of the Soviet Union, Popkov was able to take advantage of the lack of police authority to get away with his most barbaric fantasies.

Using his police uniform as a cover, he would lure unsuspecting women into his squad car where he would drive them to an isolated forest to kill them. His murders would go unabated for close to twenty years until Russian authorities finally utilized DNA evidence to match Popkov with the killings.

He was able to evade authorities because he was the authority.

Both he and his wife were police officers.

This is their story.

THE ORIGINS OF A KILLER

Mikhail Popkov was born on March 7th, 1964 in Russia. Little is known about his early life. He was a sporting youth like any other before entering the police academy. He would meet and marry Elene who was a fellow officer. The two would have a daughter, Ekaterina, who would later become a schoolteacher.

"I had a family," Popkov said. "My wife and daughter considered me a good husband and father, which corresponded to reality. I was in the service, in the police, having positive feedback on my work. I never thought of myself as mentally unhealthy. During my police service, I regularly passed medical commissions and was recognized as fit."

Accounts vary over what set off Popkov. His first known killing occurred in 1992 when he was twenty-eight years old. Most serial killers start showing anti-social behavior early in childhood. But Popkov is an anomaly in that there doesn't appear to be any early warning signs.

Popkov would claim that he never intended to become a serial killer and that it "just happened."

"I just felt I wanted to kill a woman I was give a lift to in my car," he said of his first victim in 1992.

The belief that his wife was having an affair with one of his co-workers, did seem to set him off course. His wife denied this claim vehemently but Popkov discovered two used condoms thrown in the garbage at his home. His wife claims that the condoms were used by some friends who were visiting for the night.

"I just had some reasons to suspect her," Popkov said. "I'm not looking for excuses, but this was the impetus for my future."

Fueled by a jealous rage, he began seeking out women that reminded him of his wife's sluttish ways.

Another theory is that he targeted women who reminded him of his mother. This is a typical Freudian response when assessing the motivation of serial killers who murder women...They are symbolically killing their mother.

In Popkov's case, however, this doesn't seem to hold weight. His mother would go on to the defend her son even when the evidence against him proved to be overwhelming. By all accounts, she seemed to have been a loving and doting mother to her "Mischa" as she called him.

THE ROUTINE

Popkov had an established modus operandi for abducting his victims. His targets would be women alone, often those who were drunk.

He would put on his police uniform and park his car outside discos and restaurants, waiting for a tipsy woman to come wobbling out. He would then lure her into his car with the promise of a ride.

"I could arrest you," Popkov would sometimes tell his victims. "But I'm feeling charitable. Get in and I'll take you home."

Other times, he would play the role of a cop looking out for a young woman's best interest.

"There have been reports of a man attacking women around here," he would tell the victim in a conspiratorial tone. "Let me take you home. We can't have you walking out on the streets alone."

Once inside his vehicle, however, Popkov would drive his trusting victim to an isolated forest. Once there he would force them to strip naked for him. He would become enraged, attacking them with whatever weapon he had on hand. Sometimes he used an axe, sometimes he used a knife while others he strangled to death. He would decapitate one of the victims and ripped out the heart of another.

"The choice of weapons for killing was always casual," Popkov said. "I never prepared beforehand to commit a murder. I would use any object that was in the car - a knife, an axe, a bat."

Then he would rape the victim post-mortem.

He would not go to great lengths to dump the body to avoid discovery. The attack would take place in an isolated area and he would leave bodies in the forest the side of the road and sometimes the cemetery.

Popkov nicknamed himself "The Cleaner", stating that it became his "misson" to rid the Russian streets of loose women.

"I had a double life," Popkov said. "In one life I was an ordinary person ... In my other life I committed murders, which I carefully concealed from everyone, realizing that this was a criminal offense."

"The victims were those who, unaccompanied by men, at night, without a certain purpose, were on the streets, behaving carelessly, who were not afraid to enter into conversation with me, get into my car, and then go for a drive in search of adventures, for the sake of entertainment, ready to drink alcohol and have sexual intercourse with me. Not all women became victims, but those of a certain negative behavior, I had a desire to teach and punish."

THE SOLE SURVIVOR

In 1998, he would attack a woman later referred to in the press as "Svetlana M."

Svetlana was fifteen but according to police looked older than her actual age.

She told investigators that a police car pulled up next to her and offered her a ride. Unsuspecting, she got into the vehicle where she was driven to a nearby forest.

Following his standard routine, Popkov ordered the girl to take off all her clothes. He then smashed her head against a tree and knocked her out.

He would violate her then leave her for dead.

The next day, Svetlana would be found, somehow still alive despite being completely naked in the sub-zero temperatures of the region.

She would awaken in the hospital and tell the police her story.

"She was unconscious because of severe head injuries," Nikolai Kitaev, one of the police investigators said. "Police did not start a criminal investigation for a long time despite numerous complaints from the girl's mother. Finally, Svetlana would be questioned and told in detail about her rapist-policeman and his car."

Police didn't believe her story. Svetlana, however, would identify Popkov as her attacker after she was shown a photograph of him in a police car. Police would question Popkov, who laughed it off. They also questioned his wife who stated that he was with her the whole night.

With an alibi by a trusted police officer let alone his wife, the police didn't pursue the matter any further.

"She (Svetlana) clearly confirmed it was him," Kitaev said. "But again, the police trusted Mikhail's wife - once more she composed an alibi for him and the criminal investigation was stopped and sent to the archives."

"It was enough just to perform a DNA test of this man but the police interrogated Popkov's wife who composed an alibi for her husband. Later he became more careful and carried on with his horrific crimes."

Knowing they had a serial killer/rapist on their hands, Russian investigators worked to construct a psychological profile of who their suspect could be. They surmised that he may be either a metalworker, bus driver, railroad worker or heating station engineer. They were also convinced that he may also have been a mortuary worker because so many bodies had been found at or near cemeteries.

Still, Popkov didn't have to do much to evade authorities. Russian investigators were still disorganized after the fall of the Soviet Union. He was able to elude and evade detection by simply being a little more organized than the people investigating him. It didn't take much, he knew their strengths and weaknesses...after all, he was one of them.

"There are two groups of maniacs - organized and non-organized," Russian psychiatrist Alexander Grishin said. "Non-organized maniacs are easy to catch, their crimes are quickly solved - they are people with psychiatric pathologies, who live in their own world, they are hiding from people, often untidy. Organized maniacs - Popkov is a good example - are people with high mental abilities, socially adapted, often with families, they find convenient jobs which secures them and gives time for crimes. It is a hard job to catch such a maniac, it is hard to spot such a person, even police enrollment tests are not good enough for it. The fact that only drunk women attracted him could be the result of his childhood problems and associations - his mother used to drink alcohol and often abused him. Maybe in his childhood other drunk women abused him too, and all this affected his behavior later in his adult life and led to such horrible consequences."

INCOMPETENCE LEADS TO MORE KILLINGS

The failure of the police authority to suspect Popkov coupled with his wife covering for him allowed him to murder several more women over the ensuing years.

One of those victims was Tanya Chagaeva, a 29-year old housewife with a daughter at home.

Tanya had received an invitation to go to a concert. Despite protestations from her husband who wanted her to stay home, Tanya wanted to take in the experience.

"It happened 15 year ago but the pain does not go away - it was me who presented Tanya a ticket to go to a concert, and she was killed after attending it', Viktoria Chagaeva, Tanya's sister said.

Her husband Igor was against his wife going to the concert but she would go anyway with her girlfriend, Yulia. The two would leave their home but not return.

Igor would call Viktoria in the morning, asking if his wife had gone to stay with her sister. They both then realized that Tanya was missing.

"I got truly scared," Viktoria said. "It was the first time, she had never done this before. There were no mobile phones at that time, we could only call Yulia's parents thinking Tanya must have stayed overnight there for some reason. But Yulia's parents said she had not come home either."

The police would prove to be of little help. They told the families that they would have to wait three days before the women could be qualified as a missing person.

Later that night, a farmer would find the naked bodies of both women in a village close to Angarsk.

"It was 1am when Tanya's husband Igor and I came to the police," Viktoria recalled. "We did not tell our mother yet. Igor was absolutely devastated and only repeated - 'She was killed, she was killed'. I was shocked too, but I simply could not believe it and replied - 'what are you talking about?' Later we were told that their bodies were found next to each other, both girls were raped, cut and chopped. The experts told us that at first they were killed then raped. My elder brother Oleg went to the morgue to identify Tanya. He had flown from Moscow immediately. He felt sick when saw the body, she was so mutilated. He was almost green when he came out of there - he just could not say a word. I did not dare to go in and look."

The police had already established the chain of events. Both Tanya and Yulia had left the concert and went out for a drink with some friends. Leaving the bar, they were then offered a ride by a policeman.

"Only the fact that this bastard was in a police uniform explains why Tanya got into his car," Viktoria said. "Many people attended Tanya's funeral. It felt as if the whole town was there. Our poor mother lost her consciousness several times, she needed a lot of medicine to cope. Igor was in almost the same condition. Tanya's coffin was open, her face was not hurt. He damaged the back of her skull, and her body was heavily cut. Yulia's coffin was closed, her face was cut up and disfigured."

Tanya's mother would never be the same.

"She felt as if she had died with Tanya, life became useless for her. She lived only because she was visiting various mediums one by one, looking for the killer and wasting her money. Nobody gave her any serious information but she kept doing it. She died in 2007 aged 66 from a heart attack. I think her heart could not cope with the pain any longer."

A REIGN OF TERROR

In August of 1999, Popkov would offer a medical student a ride. He would take her to the forest and chop off her head, stabbing her six times before stuffing down a garbage chute. Later that month he approached twenty-year old Maria Molotkova. Maria was leaving work from a water pumping station when Popkov offered her a ride. Maria was unsuspecting of the police officer, just like all the rest. He would drive her to the forest, kill then violate her corpse.

In June of 2000, he would claim two of his older victims, 35-year old Marina Lyzhina and 37-year old Lilia Pashkovskaya.

Marina and Lilia worked at the same shop and left to see Marina's sister. They worked late and started to walk home around midnight. They were going to call a taxi cab but changed their minds. The night was warm and they decided to walk.

Until Popkov came along in his police vehicle and picked the women up.

Popkov would murder the women but realize that he left his police badge behind at the scene.

"I found the token (badge) right away, but saw that one of the women was still breathing," Popkov said. "I was shocked by the fact that she was still alive. I finished her with a shovel."

The two women were buried in closed coffins. Their bodies had been so mutilated that the Russian tradition of having open coffins had to be disregarded. Marina had a 14-year old daughter. Lilia had two children, a 12-year old daughter and 3-year old son.

He then targeted a music teacher at his daughter's school.

"Her corpse was found in the forest along with the body of another woman," Popkov said. "My daughter asked me to give her money, because the school was collecting to organize funerals. I gave [it to] her."

Popkov then step down from his policemen duties. He would find work in the security business, working as a guard for the Angarsk Oil and Chemical company.

FALSE CLAIMS?

Popkov would claim that he stopped killing when he became impotent as he contracted syphilis from one of his victims. There is no word if he transferred the disease to his wife as well.

The press would dub him as "The Wednesday Murder" as that was the day his victims were typically found. One detective working on the case would refer to him as a "werewolf."

It is reported that he did not stop killing after he contracted the sexually transmitted disease. Investigators are still looking at murders from the time he worked as a traveling security guard.

ARREST

On June 23rd, 2012, Popkov would be arrested in Vladivostok when he was buying a car. He had his DNA sampled along with 3,500 other police officers and his sample was matched with the semen he left behind on his victims.

"I could not anticipate the examination of DNA," Popkov said to investigators. "I was born in another century. Now there are such modern technologies, methods, but not earlier. If we have not got to that level of genetic examination, then ... I would not be sitting in front of you."

After Popkov's identity was revealed to the press, Tanya Chagaeva's sister Viktoria realized that she knew the man.

They had both competed in a biathlon at the same gym.

"I was stuck with horror when I saw the picture of this maniac in the paper and online," Viktoria said. "My sister's killer was looking into my eyes. I immediately felt as if I'd met him. Looking at him, I could hardly breathe. Some minutes later I looked at him another time and thought - oh my God, I know him! I was so shocked, I even took a knife and cut his face in the newspaper, I needed to let this horror out of me. I remember him as a tall slim man, he was always alone, with a slippery and shifty glance. I think such people just must not live. This beast took the life of my sister, who had so many happy years in front of her. I cried a lot that day, but it is time to be quiet and just wait. He will be punished by law and criminals in jail will punish him too, I am sure he will pay for all the murders one day...."

His fellow police officers who worked with him were shocked as well.

"When I read about him in the press I literally choked," said Dmitry Valuev. "Because I used to work with him and thought I knew him. He was an absolutely normal man. He liked biathlon; once on duty he shot a rapist during an arrest. There was an investigation and he was not punished, the chiefs considered he had taken fair action."

"I used to work closely with him for 5 years," Sergey Golovkin said. "He knew lots of jokes and stories, and could be soul of the party."

His own daughter was shocked. To this day, she does not believe that her father committed those murders

"I do not believe any of this," Ekaterina said. "I always felt myself as 'Daddy's girl'. For 25 years we were together, hand in hand. We walked, rode bikes, went to the shops, and he met me from school. We both collect model cars, so we have the same hobby.

"I wanted to be a criminologist, so I read a book with tips of how investigators catch serial killers and there were also basic classifications [about murderers]. Daddy doesn't fit any of these classifications - he doesn't look like some maniac."

But Ekaterina recently changed her tone, not having seen her father for over two years. She expressed a desire to "look into his eyes and understand if he really could be that killer"

Popkov's wife continues to support him although she no longer offers alibis. She would describe the charges against the husband as "fairy tales".

"We met on the Monday and Tuesday before sentencing and discussed this situation," Elena Popkov said. "He already knew that it would be a life sentence. He denied everything. Even when our daughter Katya asked him, he said, 'Katya, you understand that all these [allegations] are fairy tales. It is the system - I have worked within it, I know this system well. We have been married for 28 years. If I suspected something wrong, of course, I would divorce with him. I support him, I believe him. If he were to be released right now, I would not say a word and we would continue to live together. I love him, I support him. He did not cause me any harm for all these years. I felt safe with him."

Elena would not be the only woman to step up and defend Popkov. His mother would address the press as well and express her support.

"I cannot believe he walked alone to the forest in a police uniform," Popkov's mother said. "Where was the blood? His clothes should have been covered in blood or if he had tried to wash the blood away, the clothes would have been wet. His wife would definitely have noticed all that. He loves his family, cherishes his daughter, and he dreamed about grandchildren. He would not have done this. He will remain my son, until my death. He studied well and from the very beginning he was excellent pupil. He loved to cook, pancakes or something like this and he was very neat, like me."

But even his own mother had her doubts...

"Misha (Mikhail), give us some sign if you have done all this or not. And if so, why? It is hard to live knowing nothing. We need to know."

Popkov was initially suspected of killing twenty-nine women. Twenty-five of the women were aged 19 to 28 while four were between the ages of 35 to 40. All victims lived in Angarsk, Irkutsk.

Later, however, the Russian authorities admitted that the numbers were considerably higher after they interrogated Popkov.

"To clarify the numbers, Popkov has confessed to 59 new murders," Irkutsk Investigative Committee spokeswoman Karina Golovacheva said. "We are not counting in this total those 22 for which he was already sentenced. These cases are already closed. So there are 59 new murders. That means, if we add them to the earlier 22, it will be 81 murders in total."

Popkov would charged with an additional forty-seven murders with another twelve still pending.

"We are quite sure about the 12 other cases," Golovacheva said. "We are now gathering all the evidence. Further analysis of the evidence is underway and 'in the nearest future we can bring charges in these 12 cases' which Popkov has already admitted"

Based on Popkov's confession it appears that he is the most prolific serial killer in Russia history. He has a higher kill count that Andrei Chikatilo, aka the Butcher of Rostov, who had been convicted of over fifty-three murders. Alexander Pichushkin and Anatoly Onoprienko were convicted of fifty-two and forty-nine respectively.

But authorities now believe that he is "rationing out his confessions" as he is delaying his time in the Russian jail system before being sentenced to serve out the rest of his life in a brutal penal colony where he will be forced into hard labor.

Because he traveled so much after leaving his police job, authorities believe that Popkov is responsible for even more murders than already suspected.

Alexander Pichushkin - the Bitsa Park Maniac

*Stranger than **Fiction***

In 2010, journalist Denis Faye sat down with industry expert Pat Brown in an attempt to bridge the gap between how serial killers are portrayed in film and television and how they are in real life. Brown quickly cuts through the existing information floating around on this disparity.

> *"Faye: So what does Hollywood get right about serial killers?*
> *Brown: Very little."*

In the case of "real life" serial killer Alexander Pichushkin, known as the infamous Bitsa Maniac, the Chessboard Killer, and arguably one of Russia's most consummate serial killer, it's almost impossible to draw the line between fact and fiction. Between his mysterious past, the inventiveness of the press, and his own fabrications, Pichushkin's story requires an eye for the difference between killers from the silver screen and true monsters.

Described as a "real-life criminal profiler," Pat Brown has a lot to say about the difference between the fictional serial killers we see in movies and television and the all too real murderers we catch glimpses of in the news. In an interview with the WGA, she attempted to outline some of the most prominent errors writers make when depicting serial killers. She immediately honed in on the false complexity that writers default to in order to create drama, lamenting that such specificity is almost never the case.

> *"They're not as bizarre as the films show... [They] tend to over-profile the killer's mental state."*

In the news, Alexander Pichushkin's story has been sensationalized and stretched, the gaps in his narrative filled with fiction. Between 1992 and 2006 Pichushkin was responsible for the deaths of up to 62 people, putting him in the running for being one of Russia's most prolific serial killers. But despite this infamy and attention, there are plenty of holes in the account of his killing spree for reporters to expound and invent. Even Pichushkin's Wikipedia entry contains an entirely fictional tale of his childhood inspired solely by his title as the Chessboard Killer. This moniker may be the most popular and certainly most evocative option for Pichushkin, but it is by no means the most accurate. Those who were most affected by this slew of murders and know the most about them, locals and experts alike, all prefer the more succinct and accurate name Pichushkin had earned: the Maniac.

Creating a *Monster*

Psychologists often argue whether the monstrousness of serial killers is born or made by trauma or environment. On one hand, being able to point a finger at exactly what caused a human being to do such horrible things can be comforting, but all too often external factors are used to distance killers from blame and evoke sympathy. Brown laments that this distancing is what she is most opposed to in the portrayal of serial killers. "I've never seen a serial killer with redeeming qualities or one you can have some kind of sympathy for, like it's just a bad hobby he's got." On the other hand, a world with the potential for people who are simply born to commit heinous murders is a scary one to imagine, and given the number of environmental similarities between serial killers, one that frankly doesn't seem to exist.

Currently, the prevailing argument is that it is a combination of the natural and nurtured elements of someone's personality that react upon one another to create a psychopath, though Brown feels there is more of a conscious choice involved. "He's just pissed off at society and became a psychopath when life didn't work out his way..." In the case of Pichushkin, close analysis of his childhood, family, and early social interactions reveal many of the trademarks common in other serial killers, however, Brown's reminder of free will is an important one to keep in mind. While Pichushkin's childhood has some traumatic roots, ultimately he was not *made* into a monster—he *chose* to commit murder, and on a minimum of 52 separate occasions.

On April 9th, 1974 Alexander Pichushkin was born in Mytishchi, Moscow, and according to his mother, Natasha Pichushkina, he was a normal child as far as she could tell. Alexander, or Sasha for short, lived in a modest one bedroom apartment with his father and mother who had grown up in that same apartment. The complex is one of many on the outskirts of Moscow, a decaying remainder of soviet era infrastructure and some of the only reasonably priced housing in the area. Nicknamed *khrushchevki* after Nikita Khrushchev, the spartan public housing lacks charm and personality, but continues to serve in functionality and affordability. A mere nine months after Sasha is born, his father leaves Natasha to raise their son alone.

"I tried to raise him like a normal mother... I know now that I raised my son very poorly... [but] I can't say what I did wrong."

Besides his mother's account in a popular interview from 2007, not much is known about young Sasha's childhood. One of the few verified details of Sasha's childhood is the head trauma he incurred at the age of four when he fell backward off a swing outside the *khrushchevki* only for it to swing toward him again and strike his forehead. Immediately following the incident he spent time in an institution for the disabled, though exactly how long he stayed there is not reported. Brain injuries, specifically to the frontal lobe where Sasha was struck, are very common among serial killers. David Berkowitz, Leonard Lake,

Kenneth Bianchi, and John Gacy all suffered similar head trauma early in life, which neuroscientists link to violence and impulse control issues, as well as emotional and empathetic difficulties.

There are plenty of other mixed and unsubstantiated accounts of torment in Sasha's childhood inflicted by bullies instead of by accident, including one anecdote about a group of children ganging up on Sasha to steal his moped. A police investigator offered a possible explanation in an interview, saying that "Pichushkin" is a name with an effeminate, weak connotation, a detail that would otherwise be lost to the cultural barrier. Entrenched in a Russian cultural context often tinged with homophobia and toxic ideas of masculinity, young Sasha had his cards stacked against him. With the effeminate name, an absent father, a stint in an institution, and very few, if any, friends, he was ideal fodder for grade school bullies. Despite Pichushkin eventually outgrowing his childhood weaknesses and becoming a model image of Russian masculinity, many experts speculate that he might not be heterosexual.

Mentioned only briefly in an interview with the lead investigator, the question of the Bitsa Maniac's sexuality was quickly brushed off. Pichushkin smoked and drank, had a menial physical job stocking shelves at a grocery store, and a low voice with a gruff personality—to those surrounded by the cultural context of Russia's now-infamous homophobia, there was no possible way he could be anything but straight. Add in the brutal success of his murderous impulses and there is no hope of swaying the investigation's narrow image of Pichushkin.

His mother Natasha brought up in her 2007 interview that he never seemed to be interested in women or sex in general. His only documented emotional attachment is to a male classmate from his teens. An overwhelming majority of his victims, the people he was able to lure most easily and was most comfortable with, are all male ranging from as young as nine years old to retirement age. While there was never evidence of any sexual assault on his male victims to substantiate any of these claims, there also was a complete lack of sexual activity with his female victims as well. Based on the available, though sparse, information, it seems just as likely that Sasha lacked sexual impulse at all, and instead only had a lust to kill.

Yet another facet in the claims against Pichushkin's heterosexuality, young Sasha seemed to be heavily influenced by another serial killer, Andrei Chikatilo, whom he idolized to the extreme. Chikatilo's crimes came to light just as Sasha reached his most consciously formative years, and he kept careful track of his contemporary's every move. Chikatilo's spree of murders earned him the nickname of the Rostov Ripper, but he, like Sasha, was deemed by the press a maniac.

Finding *Inspiration*

In December of 1991 the newly liberated Russian media received news of an arrest made in relation to the series of unsolved, gruesome murders happening 117 miles northeast of Moscow, in Rostov von don. For nearly a decade the area had been terrorized by murders that were clearly linked to the same killer, who had been referred to as the Rostov Ripper. Immediately after the arrest, sensationalist news sources had yet to learn his name or see his photo, but had a brief summary of his crimes. His signature was stabbing, usually in excess of 30 times, gouging of the eyes, sexual assault, and evisceration; accused of 53 counts of murder in this style, the man whose name would later be learned became simply *the Maniac*. The public did not lay eyes upon the monster that they knew so little about until he appeared at the first day of his trial on April 14th the following year.

Just five days after Sasha's eighteenth birthday the media is suddenly saturated with the face of the Rostov Ripper, now revealed to be Andrei Chikatilo. His sallow face is pictured from behind iron bars throughout the trial, specially put in place of the usual plexiglass box, to protect him from the often hysterical and retaliatory relatives of his victims. These attacks were not the only noteworthy outbursts of the trial: Chikatilo and the judge, Leonid Akubzhanov, remained combative toward each other throughout the proceedings, with Chikatilo refusing to cooperate. Ignoring questions posed by the prosecution, Chikatilo's original well-spoken demeanor devolved into a show-stopping display of chaos, singing socialist anthems and exposing himself to the jury in an attempt to be deemed unfit to stand trial.

As the trial continued into the summer, news outlets revealed more of Chikatilo's gory past, full of sexual assault while in his teaching position, torturous excess during his killings, and the numerous occasions he was apprehended, questioned, or suspected before his final arrest. Sasha followed all of these stories with more than the morbid curiosity typical of a boy his age. He clipped articles from the papers and kept photos of Chikatilo's face, images with captions that described him as a "shaven-skulled demon" and articles detailing the horrific, decade long murder spree of *the Maniac*.

With the clarity of hindsight, Pichushkin's serial murders appear to be somewhat spawned from Chikatilo's, if not directly inspired. Teenaged Sasha was exposed to widespread press coverage of his killings and saw the attention he garnered from the public and his victims' families. He witnessed the controversy over Chikatilo's punishment, which arguably contributed to the suspension of Russia's death penalty in 1996 (notably, after executing yet another serial killer, Sergey Golovkin). At the very least, Pichushkin seemed intent on surpassing Chikatilo in number, keeping track of his alleged 61 victims with numbers pasted on his now-infamous chessboard. While journalists after the fact like to fixate on this chessboard and invent a final goal of filling it with 64 murders, Pichushkin never mentioned the board in his taped confession. Motivated only by his need to kill and desire to overshadow the Rostov Ripper, the lead police investigator doubted Pichushkin would stop when he ran out of squares.

"Pichushkin is quite an unusual serial killer he's a hunter, a typical hunter and his only motivation was to kill, there was no other motive, whatever else we might have thought."

*A New **Maniac** Begins*

On the 27th of July, Sasha takes his first step towards becoming the infamous Bitsa Maniac. Now three months after turning eighteen years old, he invites his friend and classmate Mikhail Odichuck to join him in something he has been ruminating possibly for years: to commit his first murder. For Pichushkin, this is the most intimate gesture he could possibly offer. Only a trusted friend, a confidante, someone he would deem worthy of sharing such a powerful experience of control and subversion of societal expectations could have been welcomed so wholly into Sasha's inner circle. Unfortunately for both boys, what Sasha viewed as a generous offer, Mikhail saw as a joke.

It would be easy to jump to the conclusion that Sasha held some form of fondness or affection towards his classmate Mikhail. With the seeming absence of his sexual attraction to women in combination with idolization of Chikatilo and experience being bullied as a child, their relationship could have even been interpreted as a boyhood crush. Out of 51 charges of murder and attempted murder, only three victims were female, a statistic that belies Pichushkin's gravitation toward men in general. At such an important developmental stage in his life, Sasha would be expected to display sexual and emotional attraction towards those he felt closest to at the time, namely his friend Mikhail. With over a decade of experience in examining the personalities of serial killers, specialist Pat Brown would insist otherwise.

"What people don't get is that a psychopath can portray, at certain points in his life, certain levels of affection... [but] those are just objects in his life... People are either useful, or they're in the way."

Mikhail made the mistake of getting in the way. Eventually the boy realized Sasha was dedicated to the idea of murder—and completely prepared. He knew to prey on the elderly and the homeless, strangers, who wouldn't be missed by family or valued by the police enough to warrant further investigation. He had already crafted the story of his "beloved" dog's grave in Bitsa Park as a trick to lure their victims with promise of a free drink, both lowering their victim's guard and impeding their ability to fight back. Most importantly, Sasha had discovered the manholes in Bitsa Park that fell up to 18 meters deep, full of highly pressurized currents, in which he would later dispose of twenty to thirty bodies. At exactly what point Mikhail came to the realization that Sasha was deadly serious, only Pichushkin knows—but his classmate never made it to the forest. That Monday afternoon Mikhail's lifeless body is found in the street, after dropping from a five-story balcony. Young Sasha was questioned by police, but they never suspected his involvement and ruled the tragedy a suicide with little to no other inquiry.

Prompted by Pichushkin's confession fifteen years later, a follow-up investigation examined Mikhail's body and discovered head trauma that didn't fit within expectations of impact on the ground. What they had glossed over appeared to be evidence that 18 year old Sasha had bashed in his classmate's head up to 21 times with an unidentifiable blunt object before lifting his lifeless body over the edge of the balcony to drop into the street below. Though the final result is similar to the neat, premeditated M.O. he would adopt later in life, this first murder was a crime of passion, fueled by betrayal and rage, and a moment Pichushkin would later look back on fondly.

"This first murder," he began in his televised confession, "It's like first love—It's unforgettable."

*An **Experimental Phase***

For the next nine years, Pichushkin waits. Investigators speculated that Sasha repressed his homicidal urges for as long as possible, knowing that he would not be able to stop once he started again. Pichushkin neither confirmed nor denied these claims, and has offered no other explanation for such a long hiatus. But after those nine years are up, Sasha embarks on a personal journey with an astonishing body count, to discover all the ways he can kill and all the ways he can get away with it.

Now at the age of 27, Sasha began to mix up his M.O., experimenting with weapons, victims, and body disposal. The homeless were his first choice of victims, on whom he tested out another toss over the balcony and a homemade "pen shooter" Sasha had crafted himself; Pichushkin lamented in an interview that both of these methods were over too quickly. This second falling victim was only nine years old, whose death was overlooked just like Mikhail's. As for the pen shooter incident, Pichushkin later described the murder in his confession with explicit detail, from finding a homeless man sleeping on the street, to pressing the makeshift gun to his temple in broad daylight and watching him bleed. He explained that he had seen the man as an opportunity while he was walking to work and couldn't resist.

Eventually he moved on to victims who needed to be lured into the cover of the park, but these still would not be the bodies found by police and attributed to the Bitsa Maniac. The story Sasha told many of his victims centered on a "beloved" deceased dog, whose grave, he told them, was in the park. He would offer a drink of vodka over the nonexistent burial site to distract and relax them; little did they know that the spot he lead them to was strategically located by one of the manholes he had discovered in his youth. Sasha would then bash their heads on the manhole cover, only to open it and lift their inebriated or even unconscious bodies over the edge. His story varied slightly each time, and he continued to use opportunities like the sleeping homeless man to take advantage of poor drunks who wouldn't be missed amid his more focused strategy. Yet another distinction between fact and fiction, where news outlets attempted to fit all of Pichushkin's murders into a neat little box, Brown argues that just isn't so.

> *"[A real serial killer] doesn't have a fantastic signature with every crime, something really creepy that links every one of the crimes together ... It's very exciting, but it's not the way it is in real life. He's not always going to use the same method. He might try something else on another day, so you have to be careful of that."*

When he later told police of his use of the sewer system to dispose of the corpses, they tested its validity by dropping a mannequin inside, only for it to be immediately torn apart by the forceful currents. They also later found the body of a missing person whose death Pichushkin had claimed fault of further into the system. Pichushkin blamed the police force's ineptitude for not being able to find the bodies he had so effectively destroyed. Normally the police would have to rely on what little evidence they have to corroborate a murderer's often fantastical claims and any particulars are reliant on the trustworthiness of a murderer. In Pichushkin's case, his haste to kill left three survivors in his wake who told police and the press every minute detail.

The first to live to tell the tale was Maria Viricheva, who was pregnant at the time of her attempted murder. Pichushkin met her in a metro station on February 23rd 2002 and must have been able to recognize that she was in pressing financial need. He crafted a story of cameras he had hidden away in a manhole in Bitsa Park, offering to sell them to her at a discount so she might turn a profit. Desperate, Maria accepted and followed him into the forest. At the opening to the sewer, Maria quickly realized her mistake as Pichushkin grabbed her and beat her head against the lid, which he then opened and dropped her inside. Miraculously, Maria maintained consciousness, and gripped the slippery walls while attempting to regain some strength amidst the freezing currents. Maria estimated that she spent almost 20 hours trapped in the sewer, struggling between trying to find a way to climb out and her fading will to live. Eventually she discovered rungs that lead to another manhole and was able to climb out to safety.

In addition to Maria, 13 year old Mikhail Lobov fell victim to Pichushkin's invitation to the park for a free drink and cigarettes. Mikhail was just one of many in a crowd of leather jackets and piercings, often hanging around the metro stations, loitering in front of food stands, and drinking. Investigators were unable to find any footage of Mikhail and Pichushkin together in the metro station nearest Bitsa Park, but they still speculate that the most likely place they met would be there. Once in the park, Mikhail's story reads like just like the others—an offer of vodka over the imaginary dog's grave, head meets manhole cover, and into the sewer he goes. The exception to the normal script comes when Mikhail's leather jacket catches on a piece of metal rather high up in the sewer, and his fall is stopped before he even reaches the water. Completely unaware, Pichushkin leaves the park thinking he killed the boy. Just moments later, Mikhail is able to crawl out shaken and disturbed, but with only minor head injuries.

Possibly the most unsettling part of these survivors' stories is when they turn to the local police to report their attacker, only to be turned away. Hospitalized and having just received news that she lost her pregnancy, Maria Viricheva frantically described the entire ordeal from beginning to end, including a full description of Pichushkin's appearance. Instead of taking action, police ignored her account and instead asked for her citizenship documentation. Maria didn't have any, and the police generously offerto ignore the whole situation, leaving her injured and alone in a hospital with Pichushkin continuing his murder spree.

When Mikhail went to police, they brushed him off as a lying punk and told him to go home. Not a month later, Mikhail ran into

Pichushkin in a crowded metro station and began yelling and pulling at his hair in frustration, dragging his attacker over to a policeman standing guard and demanding vindication. The officer escorted Mikhail out of the station and told him again just to go home. Possibly even worse is the third survivor case, of a middle aged homeless man whose story has continued to be ignored and undocumented, even in the wake of Pichushkin's conviction.

Corroborated by these detailed survivor accounts, Pichushkin's confession weaves in the rest of the story. While the sewer was serving him well for body disposal, he still wasn't getting the satisfaction he was looking for. Instead of simply using the manhole cover, Sasha escalated to bringing a yellow-handled utility hammer with him to bash in the skulls of his victims before throwing them in the sewer. At this point, around thirty people had gone missing from his neighborhood. Police still weren't interested in the goings-on of the lower class, but the local gossip had begun to gain footing and Sasha wanted credit for his work.

The Hunt for the **Bitsa Maniac**

It's not until August 15th, 2005 that the police discover their first body, deep in Bittsevsky Park. The victim was a 31 year old man named Nikolai Wirogiev, who had suffered extensive head trauma and, most shockingly, had a vodka bottle lodged in the wound. Law enforcement officer Denis Adamenko was one of the first on the scene; years later he is still able to pinpoint the exact place the first body was found, and describe the scene with gruesome detail. Though he had no idea what was in store at the time of the first police-documented murder, Adamenko would continue working on the case from the first body to Pichushkin's trial.

One month later, another man with the same injuries is found in the park. Just two weeks after that yet another body is found, and then again after only one week. Very suddenly the police began to link the murders together, realizing these stranger killings had to be the handiwork of a single killer. Though the vodka bottle signature isn't present every time, bodies begin piling up within the same age range and sex, all with substantial brain injuries. Sometimes in lieu of a vodka bottle, sticks are found in the wounds, but the reasoning for their presence remains the same: Sasha now likes to play with his victims after the fact.

Brown's interview offers some further insight into Pichushkin's newest escalation, explaining that the often-overlooked element of power is usually what creates specific signatures, such as the vodka bottle or sticks, instead of overly complex motives. "It's just that the fun ends too quickly, so instead of walking away from the body, they want to play with it because they can continue having control. *Now I'm eating you! Look at that!* It's an ongoing feeling of power."

In November of 2005 the police receive a wake up call in the form of the brutalized body and fifth victim of the unknown serial killer, a man named Nikolai Zakharchenko who was a 63 year old pensioner and an ex-cop. Like many of Pichushkin's victims, Zakharchenko lived in the same *khrushchevki* with his family, just two doors down from his murderer. Up until this point, every victim had been part of the underprivileged lower class, either homeless without family or deemed low priority by biased police. Claiming Pichushkin consciously targeted members of society that would not be missed or investigated, as some news sources allege, would be giving him far too much credit. An opportunist at heart, Sasha simply killed whenever he had the chance, with no regard for background or lack thereof, leading to the critical mistake of killing the former policeman. It's only at this point that police give the case with an accumulating body count over to an elite murder squad within the force. What the investigators don't know is that the fifth body that they've found is actually the 41st murder Sasha would later be convicted of.

By the beginning of the next year, news of a serial killer in Moscow had been upgraded from rumors among the working class to front page news. Reports from the Moscow Times warned residents of murders in Bittsevsky Park, introducing the nickname 'Bitsa Maniac' for the first time. Pichushkin's half sister Katya, who lived in the same apartment as Sasha with her husband and child, later discussed in an interview seeing a news reel about the Maniac on tv and panicking for her brother's safety. It was well known that Sasha frequented the park, but she recalls he was never afraid that there was a killer on the loose. Meanwhile, the body count continued to rise.

A **Red Herring** in Bitsa Park

In a fit of desperation, both the police and the general public began speculating wildly about the killer's possible identity. The investigation's gaze soon turned to the sanitarium looming suggestively on the edge of Bitsa Park. Many of the patients at the ward had privileges that included the freedom to leave the building during the day without aid, and police could not help but notice that the dumping grounds fell well within walking distance. Officers immediately restricted this freedom pending further inquiry; what began as a series of interviews eventually escalated into the interrogation of every single patient with the means to walk to the park. Eventually this branch of the investigation ceased, producing no leads or valid suspects.

By mid-February, a series of sensational rumors arose fueled purely by the area's vicious homophobia. Whispers citing evidence that never existed and eyewitness accounts simply looking for their five minutes of fame circulated not from the humble residents of the *khrushchevki,* but from the panicked upper middle class. Suddenly past visitors to the park came out of the woodwork, claiming they saw the killer fleeing through the trees and describing him as a man in women's clothing and a wig. Yet another piece of gossip spread claiming some of the bodies had been raped and found with lipstick marks all over the face, neck, and body.

Demonstrating they are not immune to the rampant homophobia and transphobia of the people they protect, local police claimed an innocent victim to their witch hunt. Late at night on February 20th, someone whom the lead investigator later described as a middle aged transvestite was seen in Bitsa Park by police canvassing the area and whose mere presence was immediately deemed suspicious.

Accounts of what followed vary greatly, with many sources glossing over the resulting exchange entirely. Claims range from the suspect attempting to flee, mysteriously breaking free of handcuffs, to pulling a knife that was never found and threatening the policemen directly. One source described nearly 200 officers being called to the scene to detain this one person. The most agreed upon and substantiated elements of that night seem to be that the suspect had a hammer in their bag, and one thing led to another that resulted in police shooting the suspect in the leg and requiring hospitalization. It was later found that their "suspect" had corroborated, air-tight alibis for each of the murders and had done nothing wrong; the hammer had been for protection against the Maniac.

Apprehending the **Culprit**

Two months and nine bodies later, the police finally caught their break in the form of Marina Moskalyeva, the first victim since young Mikhail with direct ties to Pichushkin. Marina was a single mother to her 15 year old son and worked full time at the same grocery store as Sasha. Not only had they worked together, but when questioned after the fact, Marina's son described Pichushkin as her boyfriend and had met him before. Thanks to a subway ticket in the pocket of her jacket, police were able to easily find footage of Pichushkin meeting Marina at a metro station just outside Bitsa Park on the day of her murder. In case that had not been enough, Marina had left a note with her son saying she was going for a walk in the park, naming Sasha Pichushkin and even listing his phone number in case her son needed her.

Marina had known there was a killer at large in Bitsa Park and went anyway; likewise, Pichushkin knew Marina had left a note with his name and number, and still killed her. The man Marina knew—the shelf-stocker who lived with his mother, a man's man, a smoker and a drinker, her coworker—seemingly posed no threat. She had known him, trusted him enough to introduce him to her son. In the case of Pichushkin, investigators suggested that he craved the attention of getting caught, purposefully choosing a victim that would lead to his arrest. What seems more likely based on his confession, is that when given the opportunity to kill Sasha simply couldn't resist.

Within hours of being apprehended, Pichushkin confessed to not only Marina's murder and the twelve others the police are aware of, but claimed he had killed as many as 63 people. Plying him with sandwiches and cigarettes, detectives finally begin to understand the scope of the disappearances and consequent murders in and around the ignored *khrushchevki*. Following standard procedure for murder cases, Pichushkin is taken to the scene of the murders to reenact them on film, eventually to be used as evidence in his trial. Due to the extensiveness of his crimes, what is typically only a few hours of video continues on for nearly 40 hours filmed over the course of a month.

While Pichushkin's trial is much less of a spectacle than that of his idol, Chikatilo, it is still well publicized and attended by an aggravated crowd of his victims' families. Despite his fluctuating claims of 62 to 64 murders, the official charges brought to trial on September 13th are for 49 counts of murder and 3 attempted murders. Where police had ignored the voices of the lower class and their accounts of missing friends and families, the press steps in. With Sasha's quiet and undocumented past, journalists take statements from family members of victims, neighbors from Pichushkin's building, even random members of the community, stitching together a story for the Chessboard Killer, no matter how fabricated.

The most notable aspect of the trial was possibly the lack of controversy surrounding such a large and well-reported case. With very little deliberation, Pichushkin's psychological evaluation deemed him sane, stating that "his actions were purposeful and consistent... he was aware of what he was doing." After meeting for only three hours, the jury unanimously ruled Pichushkin guilty on all counts. Pichushkin's defense team filed an appeal within weeks but it was denied immediately. The first fifteen years of Pichushkin's life sentence were ordered to be spent in solitary confinement in a northern high security prison, where he remains today.

Despite the severity of his sentence, the prosecutors and the family of his victims are still divided in their opinions of his punishment. The chief prosecutor told the press immediately after the trial let out that he believed that "justice has been done... He received the punishment that he deserved." In contrast, Tamara Klimmova, whose husband fell victim to Pichushkin, demanded more.

> *"He should be handed over to the public for punishment rather than allowed to live in prison at our expense."*

Now nearly nine years into his sentence, Pichushkin continues to serve out his punishment in solitary confinement. Sasha will be 44 years old when he integrates back into communal prison life, just another member of Russia's growing prison population of almost six hundred fifty thousand people, lost in the crowd of the criminal justice system.

ONLINE DATING KILLER : THE TRUE STORY OF MARK TWITCHELL

AMY DELANEY

Mark Twitchell

"I was tentative about reaching out because I thought I couldn't offer much and doubted anyone could look past my reputation to the see the human being. But trying is definitely worthwhile if it means finding just one meaningful, mutually fulfilling friendship. My crime doesn't define who I am or represent me at all. I've made some terrible, regrettable choices in the past and I've come to terms with the consequences. Now I seek to infuse purpose into my life. Connection is a huge part of that. My creative engine never slows, so I produce artwork constantly and craft novels or screenplays to manifest my relentless imagination. I'm insightful, passionate and philosophical with a great sense of humor. I enjoy tennis, chess and clever story telling. I love the rain and the music of artists like Sia, Jackie Evancho and Arcade Fire. I'm looking for an interesting, intelligent, open-minded, delightfully imperfect woman to relate to and share amusing observations with...as well as potentially a long weekend every few months if it gets there naturally."[1]

Online dating has become the norm for many of us. Busy lives, children, sometimes working two jobs in order to provide as a single parent, means that it's not so easy anymore to meet people in 'real life'. But this profile is different – this profile belongs to prisoner Mark Twitchell, a convicted murderer who used one of the most popular dating sites around, *PlentyofFish.com*, to lure his victims to an empty garage, where he hoped to satisfy his lust for blood. His first attempt went wrong, and his victim got away – the next was not so lucky.

Mark

Not a lot is known about Mark Twitchell's childhood. He was born on July 4th, 1979, in Edmonton, Canada, to Norman and Mary Twitchell[2]

By all accounts, he had a normal, loving upbringing,[3]but life outside the family home was apparently significantly different and quite difficult for the boy.

Twitchell went to St Cecilia's Junior High, and then Archbishop O'Leary High School, where he was frequently teased and ostracised by his classmates and peers. His nickname was 'Twitch Hell', and the other kids would steal his glasses and taunt him with them, keeping them just out of reach in order to make Twitchell grab for them again and again.

One of his classmates recalled how he would feel unable to help Twitchell as the other kids bullied him.

"I felt really bad for the guy...I remember my dad taught him how to shoot a gun for the first time on a class trip - he could barely hold it after 10 shots. Now people think he's a killer. Unreal."[4]

He graduated from Archbishop O'Leary High School in 1997 and went on to study Radio and Television Arts at Northern Alberta Institute of Technology. He graduated in 2000, and married his first wife, Megan Casterella, on January 4th, 2001. The couple met in an online chat room. The young bride wanted to be close to her sister, so, after they married the young couple moved to Davenport, where Megan enrolled at Palmer College.

At first, Twitchell worked for American TV as a salesman in Davenport, before being transferred to Peoria, some 100 miles away. The couple moved so that Twitchell could be closer to work - however, he still spent much of his time in Davenport.[5]

The marriage lasted four years.

First Divorce

It was not only Megan who took her leave of Twitchell – after working with the company for two years, American TV 'released' him without revealing the reasons why.

The marriage had not been a happy one. When Megan filed for divorce in 2004, Peoria court documents showed that her husband had *"been found guilty of extreme and repeated mental cruelty."* That, plus the spiralling debt of $40,000, spelt the end of the marriage for Megan and Mark.

Although the marriage had been rocky and, by all accounts, abusive, their former landlord, Jody Kimbrell, said the couple had been model tenants – rent was never late, the unit was kept clean and tidy, and there were never any complaints from neighbors. Even after the pair divorced, and Twitchell moved out of the matrimonial home and into another unit in the complex, there was never any cause for concern.

Kimbrell even recalled that there was no friction after the divorce. *"They didn't really speak to each other, but they were cordial."*

Mark Twitchell was an avid Star Wars fan and used to buy and sell merchandise on the internet prior to his divorce.

"Star Wars dolls, paraphernalia, suits, outfits, he had it all – and he bought and sold them constantly...There was Stars Wars stuff all over the unit, but hey, whatever people collect, they collect."[6]

Twitchell's interest in Star Wars wasn't confined to the merchandise, however. Even after he moved to Peoria he remained a member of the 'Quad-Cities Jedi Order', a fan club dedicated to the films. He was also actively involved in Star Wars online forums and groups and was a prolific poster on the boards.

The Dark Side

Although Twitchell's obsessions seemed to be centered around the Sci-fi genre, his wife, Megan, caught glimpses of his more sinister side.

In a book written by investigative journalist Steve Lillebuen, Megan says *"He kind of had that really dark, secretive side...He would make comments like, 'You can't handle what goes on in my mind."*

That dark side stayed relatively hidden, apart from the few glimpses Megan caught, for quite some time. Twitchell's time on Star Wars forums had cemented his belief that he should make a fan film about the franchise, and he became more and more immersed in the fantasy, making costumes and spending time at Star Wars conventions.

It was during his marriage to Megan that Twitchell found a new way to have fun. Already well-versed on the internet through both his Star Wars forums and internet dating sites, Mark Twitchell started making up false profiles and tricking people into talking to him – a 'skill' which would eventually lead to something far darker.[7]

However, science fiction had a rival for Twitchell's attention, in the form of 'Dexter' – a TV show about Dexter Morgan, a blood-spatter analyst with Miami Police Department by day, and serial killer by night. Mark Twitchell had found his idol.

Jess

In the fall of 2005, Mark met Jess on the dating website, PlentyofFish.com, and in January 2007, Jess became the second Mrs Twitchell.[8] The honeymoon period came to an end that same year when Twitchell and a former girlfriend made contact on facebook.

Traci Higgins had met Mark Twitchell at the Northern Alberta Institute of Technology where they both studied, in 1997. Their friendship developed, and the pair became a couple. However, Twitchell's dishonesty caused problems in the relationship, and Traci broke it off. But in 2007 they found themselves back in touch – Traci, like Mark, had gone on to marry someone else, and again, like Mark, had gone through a divorce.

The fact that Twitchell had remarried did not deter the former girlfriend, and the pair met up for dinner, with the evening ending with 'a long kiss'. Contact continued between Mark and his mistress throughout 2008, and on October 10th of that year, the pair met up to go to the movies.

The movie, *Quarantine*, was not enough to hold their attention, and instead of watching the screen the couple 'made out' until it was finished, at around 5 pm, after which Traci went home alone. Twitchell, however, had other things on his mind,[9] something Traci would find out about later.

House of Cards

Mark Twitchell still saw himself as a big-time movie producer and harboured dreams of making it big in Hollywood. Towards the end of

September 2008, Twitchell gathered together a film crew, along with a few actors he had found through online casting-call agencies, and they all met at a converted garage he had rented and turned into a filming studio.

Twitchell, now into his third season of Dexter, had written a short film based on the show and called it *House of Cards*. Inspired by the character, Twitchell had turned the garage into his own 'kill room', complete with metal chair, and walls covered in plastic. The story centered on a writer who would lure other men by assuming a false identity on internet dating sites, pretending to be a woman. The killer would arrange to meet the 'dates' at home, where he would jump them, and bind the men with duct tape to the metal chair, which was bolted to the concrete floor. Before murdering the men, he would obtain their banking details and passwords, and once he had their information would brutally kill them and dismember their bodies before stuffing their body parts into plastic bags.

In the eight-minute movie, the killer bought time by using the passwords obtained before the killings to send emails and social media messages to the victims' friends and family, explaining their unexpected absences on a longer stay vacation.

The actor who played the part of the murderer, Robert Barnsley, flew in from Toronto on the promise of a $30,000 cheque for Twitchell's next movie, for his part in *House of Cards*.

The 20-year-old was more than a little surprised by the set-up when he arrived at the garage. The props were real – sharp knives, a stun gun, and a metal table. Although there had been mention of using real blood from a butcher, it was finally decided that they would use corn syrup and red food coloring.

Chris Heward was the actor playing the part of the victim. While he was duct taped to the chair, Barnsley was given a real sword and told to simulate sticking the sword into Heward's chest.

"I twisted the sword to the side, making it look like it was being twisted inside him. I would grind my teeth in the pleasure of killing him."

Heward found the experience unnerving. *"It was very uncomfortable...I was freaking out...I really didn't know these guys. At the time, I was thinking it was really dumb not to bring my agent or anybody with me."*

The final scene of the movie saw the killer sitting at a computer and closing down a fake woman's profile, before putting away a hockey mask – the same kind as had been worn during the murder. When his wife asked him how the story was coming along, the killer replied *"Really well, sweetie...It's true when they say the best way to succeed is to write what you know."*[10]

Lies

Earlier that year, in the Spring of 2008, Twitchell had found himself a job in sales. However, his obsession with his film-making took over and he stopped going to work, without telling Jess. By the time she found out, five months later, the marriage was already deeply in trouble. Their daughter had been born at the beginning of the year, and Jess was sleeping upstairs with the baby while Mark slept downstairs in the basement. He had set up a company called Xpress Entertainment, and was living off the investments backers had put into the company.

When Jess asked her husband what he was working on, in September 2008, he told her it was a film about a man who is having an affair. The premise of the story, he had told her, was that the man had arranged to meet a woman he had met online while telling his wife he was going to the gym. The woman is then attacked and murdered by a masked assailant. When Jess learned that the ending involved the woman being decapitated, she objected and asked her husband to change it.

Jess was quickly learning about her husband's darker side.

The couple, in a bid to solve their marital difficulties, were attending regular counselling sessions together, and Mark was seeing a psychiatrist by himself every Friday evening. On Friday, October 10th, Jess called her husband to ask where he had gone after his session. In a bizarre likeness to the script Jess had objected to, Mark told her he was at the gym. Jess, however, already knew that the gym they both used was closed, and told him so. He then claimed that he was at a different one.

Although the similarities to his story line were striking, there was one major difference. Although Twitchell had, indeed, spent the afternoon with a woman – his mistress Traci Higgins – he had a different kind of rendezvous planned for the evening.[11]

Gilles Tetreault

What nobody realized, however, was that Twitchell had already blurred the lines between fact and fiction. The filming at the end of September had clearly triggered something in his head, giving him the desire to feel what the killer felt.

The filming of the graphic murder scene had gone well, and everyone in the crew was happy with the results – everyone except Twitchell himself. It hadn't gone unnoticed by several members that the director had gone quiet towards the end of the shoot, and only seemed to cheer up when the crew decided that the remaining scenes were superfluous and that they should call it a wrap.[12] Was that when the seeds were finally sown in Twitchell's mind?

It could well have been, because, only a few days later, Twitchell came face to face with his first victim.

36-year-old Gilles Tetreault had been chatting to a woman named Sheena on the dating site, Plentyoffish.com, and she had asked him to meet her for a date. On October 3rd, 2008, Gilles arrived at the garage where Sheena had arranged to meet him. Although he felt it a little odd, he understood her concerns about not wanting to give her address out to a stranger. But when Tetreault entered the garage, there was no sign of the pretty blond woman he had arranged to meet. Instead, he was confronted by a masked man who attacked him with a stun baton, before pulling a gun on him and ordering him to lie down. As the assailant began to duct tape his victim's eyes closed, Tetreault was terrified.

"I started tearing up. A lot of things were going through my head. When they say your life flashes before your eyes, that's what it was. My family. They may never see me again."

Unsure of whether his attacker was going to rob him, rape him, or murder him, Tetreault decided to fight back with everything he had.

"I decided I'd better fight back. I'd rather die my way than his way."

As he began to fight, Gilles grabbed the gun, and, feeling the plastic, realized it wasn't a real firearm. That realization gave him strength, and he took hold of the first thing he could lay his hands on – a pair of handcuffs which had been lying on the floor.

As Tetreault fought for his life, his attacker began to rain punches down on him, but he managed to make it outside. His legs were shaking so much that he was unable to run, though, and he had only made it as far as the pathway when he felt himself being dragged back inside once more.

Tetreault knew that if he was taken back inside the garage again he would be dead, so, gathering all of his strength, the 36-year-old man fought back, again managing to break free from the man who was wearing what he could now see was a hockey mask.

Fortunately for Tetreault, a couple were walking by with their dog and stopped to see what was happening. As Tetreault pleaded with them to help him, the attacker, still wearing his hockey mask, told them everything was ok and that they were just fooling around. The couple left without helping, but it was enough to unnerve the assailant, and he turned and fled, leaving Tetreault to escape.[13]

Once home, Gilles decided to report the attack to the police and logged on to the internet to bring up 'Sheena's' profile as proof. However, the profile had already been deleted and now, Gilles realized, he had no proof of what had taken place, so he made the decision not to, for fear of not being believed.

Gilles Tetreault had had a lucky escape, but it wouldn't be long before he understood exactly how lucky he had been.

Johnny Altinger

Although Mark Twitchell had failed in his quest for murder, the incident with Gilles Tetreault had only strengthened his blood lust. He would try again, and this time he wouldn't fail.

On October 10th, 2008, only a week after his first attempt, Twitchell once again went online in search of his next victim. Plentyoffish.com yielded new prey, and Twitchell struck up a conversation with 38-year-old Johnny Altinger. This time, Twitchell portrayed himself as 'Jen' a 5'6" pretty brunette, who described herself as a hopeless romantic. She invited Johnny to meet up with her that evening, and naturally, he agreed.

Once again, directions to the garage were emailed. In his eagerness to meet Jen, Johnny arrived at the garage 45 minutes early, and, seeing the door open decided to go on in. Mark Twitchell was caught unawares – his kill room wasn't ready and he wasn't prepared when he heard Altinger call out Jen's name. As Johnny ducked under the plastic sheeting, he saw Twitchell, who told him that Jen had said she would be right back. Altinger knew something was terribly wrong, and made to leave, instructing Twitchell to tell Jen that he would come back later.

Twitchell was not going to let a second victim get away. After failing to kill Tetreault, Twitchell had changed his weapon of choice from the stun gun to a lead pipe, and as Altinger turned to leave Twitchell hit him over the back of the head with it, and carried on hitting, bringing it down onto Altinger's head over and over again.

Mark Twitchell had succeeded – Johnny Altinger was dead.

But the murderer wasn't finished. He had set up the garage to mirror the Kill Room in Dexter, complete with a metal table. It was on to this table that Twitchell dragged Johnny's lifeless body.

And it was there that he set about methodically dismembering him, relishing the feeling as he cut, sawed, and hacked his way through skin, muscle and bone, piece by piece.

Mark Twitchell finally had his taste of blood, in every sense. As he stood with his hands drenched in his victim's blood, he calmly ate a candy bar, before continuing with his gruesome task.

Of course, once the body was dismembered it had to be disposed of. Twitchell placed all of the body parts into plastic bags and put them in the trunk of his car. His first plan of action had been to drop them off the bridge into the river, but he changed his mind and instead threw them into a sewer.

His job was still not finished though. In order to deflect suspicion, Twitchell broke into Altinger's apartment and found his laptop. Altinger was still logged in, which made Twitchell's job so much easier, and he sat down in his victim's chair and sent emails to Johnny's friends, telling them he, 'Johnny', had run away to Costa Rica with a girl he had met, and that he would be gone for a couple of months.

He sent a further email to Johnny's workplace, telling his employer that he had resigned with immediate effect.

Twitchell stole the laptop – happy that he had covered his tracks.[14]

The Investigation

Unfortunately for Twitchell, the emails he had sent to Johnny's friends didn't convince them. This behavior was uncharacteristic for the man they knew.

They took the emails to the police, insisting that something had happened to their friend, but at first, the police weren't interested. After all, Johnny Altinger was a 38-year-old man and as such was free to come and go as he pleased. He had no history of mental illness, he wasn't considered a high-risk, and he lived alone, so for a few days, the police did nothing.

His friends would not give up, though, and eventually, the police agreed to investigate. The case made its way from desk to desk, and department to department, until it landed on the desk of Detective Bill Clark, a homicide detective, Clark was unimpressed – in a city with high crime he was a busy man, but nevertheless he decided to take a look, and attended a briefing about the case.

Johnny's friends had continued to receive emails from Johnny.

"I've met an extraordinary woman named Jen who has offered to take me on a nice long tropical vacation...We'll be staying in her winter home in Costa Rica, phone number to follow soon."

However, that phone number never arrived, and the only way Johnny's friends could contact him was via email, facebook, or MSN messenger. When they questioned why they couldn't reach him by phone they were told that the reception was bad.

It was lucky that Johnny had had the foresight to give the directions to the garage to a friend before he set off on his date. The police were able to track down the place and discovered that, rather than a woman named Jen, the house to which the garage belonged was rented by Mexicans, and that the tenant of the garage was a local filmmaker who was using the garage as some sort of studio.

The police interviewed Twitchell – he was cooperative and helpful and seemed genuinely bemused by the case. When the garage was searched, Twitchell was asked when he was last there, and he told officers that he hadn't been there since September. However, one of the officers noticed a lot of cleaning supplies on the table, along with a receipt. The receipt was dated October 15th. Twitchell played it down, claiming that he had forgotten that he had stopped by briefly to drop off some cleaning supplies, which he had forgotten about until then. Something didn't sit quite right. Detective Clark felt that it was too great a coincidence that a man had disappeared on a first date from the exact same place that was being used by a filmmaker. Twitchell was interviewed a second time.[15] The police decided to bring in crime scene investigators and asked Twitchell if he would give permission for them to go over the garage for evidence. He readily agreed, but then offered up some new information. He claimed that, on the night of Altinger's disappearance, he had been approached by a man who asked him to buy his red Mazda for $40. Officers followed Twitchell's directions and found the car about a mile away. The car was registered to Johnny Altinger, and police now had the connection between him and Twitchell.[16]

Apart from the Mazda, Clark found several more flaws in Twitchell's story, but he didn't have enough evidence to hold him, so he was released. Clark had read the scripts the crew had been working on, and had started to see similarities between the story and the disappearance. Although he didn't have enough to keep Twitchell there, Clark did have sufficient cause to seize Twitchell's car.

That was when his story began to unravel.

The Pontiac Grand Am was searched, and police found Twitchell's laptop, along with traces of blood, both in the trunk and on a knife which was next to the laptop. The computer was taken by technicians to see what could be found, and Clark was presented with a 42-page document which had been recovered from the deleted files, entitled 'The SK Confessions'. The first paragraph read: *"This story is based on true events. The names and events were altered slightly to protect the guilty. This is the story of my progression into becoming a serial killer."*

As Clark read on, he discovered that what the police had uncovered was a diary of the murder of Johnny Altinger. It detailed the dating ruse, the murder, and the intention of repeating a murder every Friday night. It also revealed the earlier attempted murder of Gilles Tetreault. However, the one detail Clark wanted more than any other was the whereabouts of Johnny Altinger's body – a detail which Twitchell had failed to record.[17]

Twitchell, still a free man, was put under 24-hour surveillance, with police concerned that he would kill again. On October 20th, 2008, ten days after Altinger's murder, they obtained a search warrant, and as they searched his house Jess took their daughter and left. She found her husband at his parents' house and told him the police suspected him of murder. She also questioned him about an incident which had happened recently, when she had caught Mark looking at a website which offered married people the chance to have affairs. At the time, Mark had told his wife that it was research for a freelance article, but when she confronted him again at his parents' house, Mark confessed. He had even been so devious as to hire an actor to play the part of an editor should Jess decide to check out her husband's story, a fact he admitted that day.

Jess left Mark there and then, and the next time she saw him was when she gave evidence at his trial.[18]

During the search of the couple's St. Albert home, they uncovered several pieces of incriminating evidence. A pair of Mark's recently washed jeans which still had traces of blood on them, and some blank postcards of Costa Rica – the place Johnny Altinger had supposedly gone with 'Jen'.

The search moved on to the garage, which the detectives now decided warranted a much closer look. Unlike Dexter, Twitchell hadn't managed to remove all traces of blood, and not only was there blood in the cracks on the table but they also found a large amount of blood spatter on the door, and less than two weeks later the blood from the garage, as well as the blood found in the trunk of Twitchell's car, was proven to be that of Johnny Altinger.

His Arrest

The police had all the evidence they needed, and on October 31st, 2008, Mark Twitchell was arrested for murder.

When Gilles Tetreault saw the news coverage, he realized that it was the same attacker, and came forward with his story. However, throughout all of their investigations, the police still had no idea where Johnny Altinger's body had been dumped. They brought Twitchell back to the garage in the hope that it would prompt him to reveal the location of his victim's remains, and on June 10th, 2009, he finally revealed where police could find the body by giving them a detailed map leading to the sewer where he had hidden the body parts.

The Trial

On March 16th, 2011, Mark Twitchell's murder trial began. He took the stand as the only witness for the defense, and told a story about how he had set Johnny Altinger up in an elaborate hoax to gain publicity for the movie. When Altinger realized this, according to Twitchell, he became irate and a fight ensued. A fight which led to Altinger's death. It was, Twitchell claimed, self-defense.[19]

A key piece of evidence in Twitchell's trial was the 42-page document, 'The SK Confessions'. He claimed that the initials 'SK' stood for his favorite author Stephen King – when in fact, it was believed that it stood for 'Serial Killer'. The jury heard the document read out loud, listening to graphic details of the killing, and the subsequent dismembering, of Johnny Altinger. There were some details which were held back, as they were thought to be too distressing for the members of the jury to hear. One such passage described how, when Twitchell cut off Altinger's head he played with it as if it was a puppet.

"I grabbed his jaw with my gloved hand and moved it while making a funny voice to make it look like it was talking, and chuckled to myself at the total silliness of it all."

Other details of the document, which Twitchell insisted were fictional, provided further insight into his psyche. He described the moment he cut open his victim's torso and watched the internal organs becoming displaced.

"If I had a sense of smell this might be disgusting for me. But I only find it fascinating...Most people fantasize and it only ever stays a fantasy. They don't have the disposition or the stomach to go all the way with their dark urges. But I do."

Talking of killing in a more general sense, Twitchell went on:

"I do not have any reservations about disposing of the negative people in this world who deserve a one-way ticket to the afterlife if such a thing exists."[20]

On April 12th, 2011, Mark Twitchell was found guilty of murder and sentenced to life in prison with no chance of parole for at least 25 years.

It was decided not to pursue the charge of the attempted murder of Gilles Tetreault, as it would not add to the maximum sentence he had already received.

Twitchell continued to cause controversy from inside Saskatchewan Penitentiary where he is serving his sentence, by buying a flat screen TV for his private cell, on which he was able to continue watching the show 'Dexter' – the same show which had inspired him to murder Altinger and attempt to murder Tetreault.[21]

As Bill Clark put *it "He's reliving his fantasy whenever he's watching that show...It's ridiculous to think that he would be allowed to do that. Maybe he's refining his skills?"*[22]

A worrying thought for everyone, but perhaps none more so than an ex-employer of Twitchell, who was mentioned in the 'SK Confessions', who was described as *"a twisted old fart who hated life and everything in it. I owed it to the world to remove him from its glorious surface and would take my chance when I was ready."*[23]

THE SUNSET STRIP KILLER: The True Story of Carol Bundy

73

Jessi Gaines

Born Carol Mary Peters on August, 26, 1942, Carol Bundy's childhood, much like her adulthood, was spent pursuing a desperate need for attention and validation. Bundy's ability to idealize or overlook any unpleasantness made her a perfect victim for manipulators and abusers looking for a potential victim – a talent she picked up early on to deal with the abuses of her parents, Charles and Gladys Peters.

Bundy's memories of her childhood are happy ones – Christmases where her parents refused to let their three children miss out on the special holiday because of a lack of money, or her father's attempt to convince her that the tooth fairy had visited overnight, using a doll's feet to leave footprints through Bundy's bedroom. Bundy's mother worked as a hairdresser, but had previously been a stand-in for tap-dancer Ruby Keeler – and Bundy remembered her as a woman who exuded beauty and glamour.

Bundy, on the other hand, was awkward and unattractive, leading her mother to begin treating her as though she didn't even exist. When she was eight, Bundy came home to a locked door, and no matter how much she cried or begged her mother to let her in, Gladys refused – stating that Bundy was not her daughter. Eventually, Charles persuaded Gladys to let the girl in, but even though Bundy was allowed back into the home, her mother ignored her completely.

However, Charles was not without reproach. Gladys, who had a tendency to beat the children relentlessly with a belt, wasn't permitted to hit Bundy or her siblings – but Charles was fond of using physical abuse to assert his dominance. While Bundy remembers her father's beatings as fitting to the severity of the offense, Charles was an alcoholic who used Gladys' death as an excuse to move his assaults on his daughters from physical to sexual.

For eight months, Charles molested both Bundy and her sister Vicky, telling the girls it was their responsibility to "take their mother's place in his bed." Although Vicky maintains that the sexual abuse continued until Charles remarried, Bundy can only recall one instance where her father molested her – and described him as a good man, who loved her.

When Charles remarried, though, he began abusing Bundy more often – beating her, degrading her, humiliating her. He told her she was stupid and fat, and even that he wanted to kill her and the rest of the family – but he'd only gotten as far as the cat before his new wife had taken away his gun. After staying in foster homes, with their grandmother, and with an uncle, the girls were brought back to live with their father in California.

Desperate measures

At this point, Bundy was willing to do anything to get away from her father – and at the age of 17, she married a 56-year-old alcoholic to try and escape the abuse. Bundy had discovered how to use her sexuality and large breasts to seduce men and receive the attention she so desperately needed – but she was unwilling to prostitute herself for her new husband. When she left him, Bundy took up with another older man, a 32-year-old writer named Richard Geis.

With encouragement from Geis, who appreciated her wit and intelligence, Bundy embarked on a brief but somewhat successful writing career. However, after her father hung himself in 1962, Bundy sought comfort through sexual encounters with women. Bouncing frequently between male lovers and female lovers, Bundy was unable to find a reliable source of the attention she needed, so she eventually returned to Geis and the couple moved to Oregon.

Still, Bundy would occasionally let other men pay her for sex. Instead of urging her to seek counseling, Geis agreed to support Bundy while she attended nursing school in Santa Monica – he would pay for her education as long as she kept her grades up. In fact, Bundy was named class valedictorian when she completed the program in 1968.

It was in nursing school that Bundy met her next husband, Grant. Their relationship started off well, and continued to be relatively stable until the birth of their first son – but then, Bundy claimed, he started beating and belittling her. By the time Bundy had given birth to their second son, her eyesight had deteriorated to the point where it looked like she may have to give up nursing. Grant was faced with the prospect of being saddled with the responsibility of caring for a blind wife, as well as their two children, and grew increasingly more violent.

Bundy escaped the abusive marriage and took her two boys to a womens' shelter in 1979, where she stayed for two weeks before finding a small apartment in Van Nuys. The managers of the Valerio Gardens apartment building, Jeanette and John "Jack" Murray, took pity on the poor single mother, and Jack was frequently called on to help Bundy with issues at the apartment. Despite her husband's established pattern of cheating, Jeanette wasn't concerned about the 36-year-old month – Bundy was overweight with short brown hair, a stark contrast to Murray's typical blonde, long-legged mistresses.

The object of her affection

The kindness she saw from Murray led Bundy to develop a crush on her landlord, who took her to the Social Security office so she could receive disability payments and even to the optometrist, to get her fitted for a pair of glasses to help the single mother return to work. Murray, for his part, enjoyed having a captive audience. Good looking, with a fantastic voice, Murray had come to America from Australia to pursue a career in music – but had been unable to make it as a performer thanks to his arrogant attitude.

The two found exactly what they needed in each other, and soon began a sexual relationship. Bundy's crush rapidly became an obsession, and she started coming up with more frequent excuses to have her landlord visit her property. Her infatuation for Murray convinced Bundy that he was in love with her, too – even though he told her it would be years before he would be able to leave his wife. Bundy was well-versed in the art of overlooking negative or painful thoughts and feelings, and continued to look for ways to strengthen the connection she saw with Murray.

Regularly, Bundy loaned her landlord money and bought him expensive gifts after she received the settlement from the sale of the house she'd owned with Grant. She also opened a joint safety deposit box with Murray, and made deposits to help him cover the expenses he said he was incurring as a result of his wife's alleged cancer treatments. Still, Murray wasn't giving Bundy the attention she craved, and she started up a brief affair with Jeanette's younger brother.

In an attempt to spend some time alone with her lover, Bundy arranged a weekend for her and Murray in Las Vegas – as a "reward" for all of his help, she said. However, after the couple checked in at the hotel and took in a show, Murray left Bundy alone for the remainder of the weekend while he gambled. He returned in time to fly back with Bundy, and, hurt and upset, Bundy forgot her suitcase in Murray's van.

When Jeanette showed up at Bundy's door with the forgotten suitcase, Bundy used the opportunity to try and bring her affair with Murray to his wife's attention – thinking Murray would then be forced to leave his wife and finally be with Bundy. During their discussion, Bundy learned that Jeanette never had cancer, and she immediately confronted Murray. While Bundy was initially angry to learn that the money she'd given him to pay for the treatments had actually been used to pay off Murray's van, he calmed her down by reassuring her that his intention was still to leave his wife and eventually be with Bundy. Eventually.

However, Bundy was losing her patience. On Christmas Day, when Murray didn't show up to spend any time with her and her children, she made the decision to take matters into her own hands. Bundy attempted to bribe Jeanette into leaving her husband – which Jeanette accepted, as long as this was Murray's desire, as well. Bundy left with the hope that later that evening, she and Murray would finally be able to start their life together. But when Murray came to talk to her after discussing the situation with his wife, he told Bundy to "stay out of his life," telling her there was "no way" he would let her break up his family.

Devastated, Bundy spent a few days licking her wounds, but still turned up three days later at Murray's favorite bar, the "Little Nashville Club." Murray regularly played music at the bar, but that night, he was simply enjoying himself off-stage, dancing with his wife. Heartbroken, Bundy felt her dream of a life with Murray slip further and further away – but caught the eye of an attractive blond gentleman, who she saw watching her from across the bar.

After an evening of dancing, Bundy was taken with the stranger from the bar. Rather than taking advantage of her promiscuity, this new man treated Bundy with respect – which made her feel like a true lady, cherished and appreciated. Charmed, Bundy felt like she and Doug Clark were made for each other, and was already looking forward to seeing him again when he dropped her off at home and promised to call on her soon.

A whirlwind romance

Doug Clark waited only a few days before calling Bundy and asking to see her again. Although Bundy preferred to keep her male callers away from her children, she relented when Clark suggested he come over for dinner – and was pleased to see that her boys took to him immediately. They played, cuddled, and Clark even tucked the boys in for bed before telling them that he would be spending the night with their mother. Bundy loved the way he took care of things, and was more than willing to give him complete control.

For the first time, Bundy made love with a partner who seemed truly interested in giving her pleasure, rather than just letting her do all the work. He was an affectionate lover, telling her over and over again how much he wanted her, how much he appreciated her, how smart and beautiful she was. This was all new to Bundy, and played right into her desperate need for validation.

The next morning, however, Bundy awoke to see Clark looking concerned and anxious – his landlady was causing him grief, he said, so would she mind terribly if he moved some of his things into her apartment? Enamoured, Bundy was eager to accommodate Clark's desires, even when he requested a pair of her panties – just so he could remember her, even when they were apart. Although she felt somewhat uncomfortable with it, Bundy gave her new lover a pair of her large, cotton panties, which he promptly returned to her when he saw how big they were. Bundy was hurt, but she was still thrilled to have found such an attractive, caring, respectful man who was so interested in her.

Still, Clark's attentions weren't enough to tear Bundy away from Murray. After sending him several letters professing her deep, unwavering love for him, Bundy made another attempt to manipulate him away from his wife. This time, though, Murray refused to indulge Bundy's long-standing delusions, and told her it was finally time to move out of the building. Although reluctant, Bundy moved into a new apartment just three miles away – big enough for herself, her two sons, and her new lover.

After moving her furniture into the new suite, Murray left with his wife, but returned frequently to have sex with Bundy or persuade her into lending him more money. Not surprisingly, Murray and Clark disliked each other immediately, which Bundy interpreted as jealousy – a sign of their love for her. She told Clark how Murray had exploited her affection for him by asking for loans and gifts. Enraged, Clark demanded that Bundy cut him off immediately. She agreed, but kept the joint account open.

The perfect couple

Clark's anger over Murray's mistreatment of Bundy encouraged her enough to overlook the fact that her new live-in boyfriend wasn't covering his share of the rent, bills, or food. Bundy's new job at Valley Medical Centre, where she was now working as a vocational nurse, paid her more than enough to cover the expenses – and Bundy was content to take care of everything, as long as Clark continued to provide her with his love and affection.

Unfortunately, Clark was having a hard time keeping this up. He was proving himself to be just as self-absorbed as Murray – talking constantly about himself and his needs, with no real interest in hearing about anything Bundy brought up. However, the couple grew closer together after Clark read an article about expressing true love by fulfilling each other's fantasies. Eagerly, Clark convinced Bundy to start opening up about her own sexual desires, and he began to do the same.

Clark's fantasies were dark, but Bundy was thrilled that he was sharing these intimate thoughts with her. Bundy had a budding interest in bondage and domination, and particularly enjoyed imagining herself as Clark's captured sex slave – although in his fantasy, this role was filled by some young girl. But Clark loved that Bundy's sexual limits seemed virtually non-existent, and he pushed to include even darker subject matter, even murder. If she loved him, Clark told Bundy, she "should be willing to kill for him." Desperate to please him, she assured him that she would.

Their relationship was inconsistent. Clark would regularly disappear for hours and even days at a time, withdrawing from Bundy and drawing out her deepest insecurities. When he would eventually return, Bundy would be so relieved and happy to see him that she would say anything to convince him to stay. She also continued to react with pleasure and excitement as Clark's nighttime fantasy sharing grew increasingly sordid and graphic – even when he told her details of an ex-girlfriend's experiences with necrophilia.

A near escape

Bundy's penchant for promiscuity led her to browse personal ads occasionally, especially during Clark's frequent absences. When a posting from a well-to-do studio executive named Art Pollinger caught her eye, Bundy bravely responded to the ad. Pollinger weighed nearly four hundred pounds, but he was looking for a wife and thought Bundy a worthy prospect. Her tried-and-true method of using her past abuses to entice new lovers paid off again, and Pollinger – who genuinely enjoyed Bundy's company and thought her to be an intelligent and interesting woman – encouraged her to cut ties with Murray.

Eventually, after some persuading, Bundy allowed Polliger to drive her to the bank, where she withdrew the money she had left in the joint safety-deposit box she'd opened with Murray. Nearly $6000 was missing, and withdrawal slips were signed with Murray's name, but Bundy continued to defend Murray's deceit. Still, she took the rest of the money and put it in a chequing account where Murray would be unable to access it.

Despite Pollinger's genuine affection and desire to share his life with Bundy, the two ended up parting ways. Bundy was used to the emotional abuse she had endured in her previous relationships, and couldn't be satisfied in a healthy relationship.

Red flags

After having surgery to restore her sight, Bundy was excited at the prospect of purchasing a new car – and so was Clark, who had selected a blue 1973 Buick station wagon. Even though the car was large and difficult for Bundy to drive, since her peripheral vision was severely limited, she bought it anyway. She was desperate to give Clark everything he asked for – even guns, which he said she should have for protection. From a pawn shop in Van Nuys, Clark selected two .25 calibre Raven automatics, which Bundy was more than willing to pay for and register in her own name.

By now, Bundy's older son was starting to notice how Clark dominated his mother, and begged her to kick him out. Instead of taking her child's concern to heart, however, Bundy refused to acknowledge Clark's abuse – choosing to lash out at her son, instead. Clark and Bundy regularly beat him, and once, Clark even graphically detailed how he could kill the boy – with Bundy's son right next to him. Rather than defending her child, though, Bundy merely watched as Clark's behaviour grew more and more violent.

The couple had even stopped having sex, as Clark informed Bundy that she was too unattractive to arouse him anymore. Desperate to please him, Bundy began accompanying Clark as he picked up prostitutes from the Sunset Strip, and would watch from the backseat while he forced the usually young women to service him orally.

According to former FBI Special Agent Robert R. Hazelwood, who worked with the Behavioural Sciences Unit, men like Clark employ a specific process that can turn vulnerable women into accomplices. After identifying a woman like Bundy, desperate for attention, they use seduction techniques to reshape the woman's sexual norms – even if the woman is initially disturbed or frightened.

"These men have the ability to recognize vulnerable women and manipulate them," Hazelwood said. "The behaviour gets reinforced with attention and affection, gifts and excitement. Eventually, they are doing things that isolate them and further lower their self-esteem. All they have is this guy, so they cooperate."

Clark had plenty of experience in charming women enough to get them to do whatever he wanted, but although he had tried, he had been unable to find a suitable woman to replace Bundy. None of the other women he dated were as willing to indulge his dark sexual fantasies as Bundy was, so despite his mounting contempt for her, Clark continued to live with Bundy on and off. Bundy reassured herself that even though Clark had other girlfriends, she was the one he shared his intimate fantasies with – his feelings for her, she thought, must be deeper.

More than just fantasies

When Clark showed up at her apartment in late April, 1980, covered in blood, Bundy realized his murderous tendencies had taken a step beyond his imagination. Although Bundy chose to believe a fabricated tale Clark wove where he'd been attacked by a girl's boyfriend, the real story came out when a young prostitute named Charlene identified Doug Clark as the man who had stabbed her repeatedly with a knife after picking her up and requesting oral sex. She had been lucky to escape alive.

Bundy's suspicions mounted further when she discovered a bag of clothes and a blanket in the backseat of the Buick – covered in blood. When she confronted Clark, he told her the same kind of graphic story of sexual perversion that she'd become accustomed to hearing – only this time, the story was real.

Clark had spotted two young runaways, 15-year-old Cindy and her 16-year-old stepsister, Gina, at a bus stop. After picking them up and demanding Cindy give him oral sex, he told Bundy that he shot both girls until they were dead and then drove with the bodies to a garage he rented in Burbank. Once inside the garage, Clark said he dragged the bodies onto an old mattress and proceeded to perform acts of necrophilia on their corpses.

That night, after confessing to Bundy, Clark returned to the garage with a camera borrowed from one of his other girlfriends. After playing with the bodies again, he wrapped them in the blanket and dumped them in a ditch off the Ventura Freeway. Bundy was thrilled that he'd chosen to confess this activity to her, instead of any of the other women he was involved with.

Still, Bundy felt compelled to report the murders to the Van Nuys police. When she called the department the night after Clark's confession, she told the officer that she believed her boyfriend had committed the crime. Although Bundy told the officer some details of the case, she wasn't taken seriously, and when the call was disconnected, they assumed the "crank caller" had just hung up.

Clark started telling Bundy about other murders he claimed to have committed, including the killing of a man named Vic Weiss and the slaying of a young prostitute identified by police as teenage runaway Marnett Comer. Their relationship had become completely centered around Clark's murderous desires and Bundy's desperate need for his attention. Even though he no longer made any attempt to flatter or even be kind to Bundy, Clark had her completely under his control.

Only a few months later, at the end of June, Bundy accompanied Clark on what would be their first murder together. Cathy, who the couple picked up off Hollywood's Highland Avenue, looked about 17 years old, and agreed to perform oral sex on Clark for $30. Bundy, watching from the backseat, passed Clark the gun when Cathy failed to get him erect. He shot her, and as she lay dying with her head in Bundy's lap, Clark drove the car out into the country. Cathy was left along a gravel road near the Magic Mountain amusement park.

The very next night, Clark came home and told Bundy of another killing. He'd spotted three prostitutes working together, and convinced one of them, Exxie Wilson, to get in the Buick. After killing her and cutting off her head, Clark realized the other two women might be able to identify him if Wilson's body was found, so he went back and picked up one of the other prostitutes, later identified as Karen Jones. Clark left Jones' body near the Burbank Studios, and, after giving up on finding the third girl, returned to Bundy's apartment with Wilson's head.

They kept the head in the freezer for a few days, and Clark told Bundy how he would take it into the shower with him and push his penis into the open mouth. Eventually, Bundy cleaned the head and put it in an ornate treasure chest, which they dumped near the Studio City Sizzler where Clark had left the rest of Wilson's body. The chest was discovered almost immediately, and the relationship between Bundy and Clark grew even more strained.

The unraveling

In an attempt to gain back Clark's affections, Bundy agreed to participate in a three-way sexual relationship involving their 11-year-old neighbour, who Clark had been molesting for months. Since news of the Sunset Strip murders was spreading, prostitutes were hesitant to work alone, and it was increasingly difficult for Clark and Bundy to find anyone willing to get in their car.

Police were holding press conferences where they discussed evidence that seemed to link the cases – leading them to believe this may be the work of a serial killer. It was even suspected that the killer lived in the area, Detective Sergeant John Helvin stated to the press, "but we don't know for sure."

The stress of this ongoing investigation and Clark's lack of interest in her led Bundy to a desperate suicide attempt, and when she woke up alone at a hospital in Burbank, Bundy called Murray to come pick her up.

Bundy was willing to do anything to reignite Murray's sexual interest in her, so she started bringing her young neighbour for him to fondle. When that still wasn't enough, Bundy turned to her reliable method of playing the victim to gain her lover's sympathy – she told Murray about the murders. Although Murray didn't threaten to tell the police, Bundy knew she couldn't keep him alive. Besides, this was her opportunity to prove to Clark that she would kill for him.

On August 3, 1980, Murray climbed into the back of his van, anticipating oral sex. Instead, Bundy shot him in the head twice and stabbed him in the back half a dozen times. When she realized the bullets in Murray's head would help the police identify her gun, she cut his head off and put it in a plastic bag, eventually dumping it in a trash can near Griffith Park.

The rest of his body was found just days later, left in his van in the parking lot at the Little Nashville club. Police began questioning regulars at the club, including Murray's wife, Jeanette. Bundy was brought down to the police station and gave detectives her version of the alibi she had already discussed with Clark, which included a detailed description of a man she had supposedly sold her two guns to.

But none of this was enough for Clark, who refused to accept any of the blame for the rapidly deteriorating situation. He told Bundy that he was moving out, and left her alone while he went out to spend time with a new girlfriend. After briefly speaking to her mother-in-law and her sons, Bundy called Geis and told him about the murders. The next morning, after being berated by Clark as she drove him to work, Bundy confessed to a co-worker about the crime spree. By the end of the day, both Clark and Bundy were arrested in relation to the series of Sunset Strip murders.

According to police commander William Booth, evidence gathered during the investigation of Murray's death, along with the information collected during the ongoing investigation into the Sunset Strip murders, let them to Clark and Bundy. Bundy would end up telling the police graphic details about each murder, admitting that she thought killing was "really fun to do."

The end of the Sunset Strip

Despite the mountains of evidence connecting Clark to the killings, he continued to claim his innocence – even after he was found guilty on six counts of murder and sentenced to death. Bundy, who had initially entered a plea of "not guilty by reason of insanity," managed to avoid a similar fate by pleading guilty to her two counts of murder. She was sentenced to two consecutive terms of 25 years to life, with an added two years for using a firearm illegally.

Until her death in 2003, Bundy fought desperately to prove Clark's innocence – even as he attempted to put all the blame on her.

robert howard

ROBERT GASTON

In October 2015, a decrepit old man named Robert Howard died of natural causes in his cell. In jail he'd led a solitary existence and spoke rarely; indeed he could have been any criminal counting down his time to release except for the fact he never stood a chance of ever getting out of prison. He was serving a life sentence for murder and simultaneously under investigation for the disappearances of other young girls that he would have had access to during a horrifically brutal life of sexual crime. Robert Howard led a gruesome life of crime, rape, brutality and murder and he called himself The Wolfman.

The name certainly conjures interesting and scary thoughts; The Wolfman sounds like a movie about werewolves or a mythical creature and he actually even gave himself a new middle name, Lesarian, believed to be a mythical child killer. He also called himself the Wolfhill Werewolf and he was certainly beastly enough to be deserving of such a name, even if he was not particularly physically grotesque.

After a criminal career that spanned 40 years, this book will look at the man behind the name, The Wolfman. I want to look at what turned him into the beast he became and why he went to such grotesque lengths with his crimes. I want to look at whether there was more to the man than meets the eye, or whether he was just a psychotic murderer and rapist. I will also look at the public opinion of him and the media interest that followed the heinous crimes committed in his active years.

MURDER FILE: ROBERT 'THE WOLFMAN' HOWARD

THE EARLY YEARS

In 1944, Robert Howard was born in an unassuming part of Southern Ireland, County Laois, in a rural area called Wolfhill. He was taller than his childhood friends and had an awkward manner, but he was bright enough and did reasonably well in his classes. Interviews with school mates at an early age suggested that had no particular disposition to some of the crimes he would go on to commit, even if he skipped compulsory school whenever an opportunity presented itself. He had 8 siblings, an uncompromising mother and his father apparently drunk a great deal of alcohol in the local pubs and taverns. When he wasn't boozing, Howard's father worked in the local brick factory and brought home barely enough for them to survive.

He was already in trouble by the young age of 13 when he was convicted of burglary and sent to a young offender's institution close to his home. Unfortunately this was not the kind of institution that troublesome kids get sent to now with emphasis on rehabilitation and morals. St Joseph's Industrial School was an institution administrated by priests and brothers and the truth about such places has only recently started to emerge. It was an Irish Catholic school and the children were starved and beaten often. Former inmates have revealed the gruelling punishments dished out by the relentless priests who would frequently humiliate the children and beat them until they bled. Names were left at the front gate and each child would be just a number, a drone whose life was often damaged irreparably by the constant beatings and starvation. Talk of sexual harassment, torture and rape has also been mentioned but never proven having been so long ago, however given the record of the Catholic Church in Ireland for covering up such instances it would not take a great stretch of the imagination to guess what might have been happening. Howard later claimed to have been a victim of such sexual abuse and used this in his defence but his crimes were ultimately indefensible. For years he would be subjected to this awful regime of farming turnips and moving rocks whilst being starved and beaten and taught the word of god.

Upon release from the institution he returned to the family home but was soon thrown out on the street by his violent, alcoholic father. Wolfhill had many abandoned coal mines leftover from its mining heyday and 16 year old Robert spent many nights sleeping rough in them. He robbed and stole to sustain himself and possibly developed a bitter and twisted view of the world on those cold, lonely nights. One young boy found that his barn had been slept in and they found a blanket and some empty cans of stolen food. They also found a journal listing criminal fantasies of how Howard wanted to break into women's houses and commit violent deeds to them. This is the first inclination we have that Howard had sexually violent fantasies and wanted to commit crimes, rather than robbing and stealing to survive.

Another local source informed reporters that he was out hunting in the woods when he stumbled upon a local farmer performing sexual acts on the young Howard. This could have been Howard's way of getting money to survive. The man did not get in the way of the pair but shot his shotgun in the air in disgust. Whether he made money by selling himself is not confirmed, although he certainly continued on a criminal spiral, stealing cars and taking goods from shops until he was caught again and sent to another, equally brutal Catholic institution. This particular precursor to prison was equally renowned as a horrific institution with beatings, humiliation and abuse rife amongst the staff and inmates. One priest would later go public in saying that it was extraordinarily violent and the boys usually ended up very disturbed.

MURDER FILE: ROBERT 'THE WOLFMAN' HOWARD

THE FIRST CONVICTED SEX ATTACKS

Presumably sick of Irish Catholic institutions, and intent on a life of crime, Howard travelled to England after release from a young offender's institution for the second time. Given the harsh conditions imposed upon him during these brutal periods it would be only logical to assume he was a fairly unstable individual at this point. He continued his life of crime in England and robbed and stole to survive, living rough whenever he could not find a place to stay.

Shortly after his 21st birthday, his crimes escalated into sexual abuse as he broke into a London home and pretended he was a doctor, ordering a young girl to undress. He attempted to rape the 6 year old girl and left violently beat her, almost killing her. He fled the scene after he heard someone coming but he escaped. Strangely, he returned to exactly the same house soon after to try again with the same girl but he got caught. His sentence seems insanely lenient as he received 9 days in borstal, and then as was common at the time, he was deported back to Ireland. The governments of both countries seemed eager to avoid media attention on keeping prisoners of the other nationality, given the troubles north of the border in Ireland, which resulted in the ridiculous 9 day sentence and subsequent deportation and release. Howard had a taste of England and chose not to stay in Ireland for long.

It seems ridiculous that a man caught red handed attempting to rape a 6 year old would have been released after 9 days in borstal, and much investigation was done into why his sentence was so lenient. Much of this centred on the political ramifications of the UK holding Irish nationals as prisoner. Needless to say, this should have been the end of the story as the Irish authorities obviously did not realise the sincerity of the situation and what heinous deeds the man they released would go on to commit.

MURDER FILE: ROBERT 'THE WOLFMAN' HOWARD

CONTINUED LIFE OF CRIME

Upon his return to England, Howard was now an extremely dangerous man intent on a life of crime and sexual assault. In 1969, the same year as the Apollo moon landing, Howard found himself in Durham, and continued on his path of destruction. He broke into a house and attempted to rape a young woman, causing her immense physical injury before she escaped and ran down the road, naked and screaming in a fit of hysterics. In a fit of lustful rage he chased her but neighbours managed to get the better of him and he was promptly arrested. After a very short court session he was sentenced to 6 years imprisonment in Frankland Prison, despite the possible political ramifications. The court heard at this time of the life of crime and the judge decided that a spell in an institution was what was needed. Early release from a jail term is usually reserved for those who demonstrate good behaviour, although Howard's period in adult prison seems to have been filled with fights and bad behaviour, having assaulted a female police officer and beaten her badly before being dragged away. Despite this, or perhaps they just wanted rid of him, Howard was released from Frankland and sent back to Ireland where he did stay for a while.

Documents were much easier to forge in the 1970's and Howard had obviously gotten a false identity as he found a job in County Cork, working on a factory near the coastal town of Youghal. He called himself Lesley Cahill but although he was now employed, he would soon resume a life of crime that he had been following since a young age.

It is very easy to blame the authorities in such cases but it really looks as though something should have been done to at least attempt to evaluate and rehabilitate the Howard before he was released and allowed to go on to commit murder.

MURDER FILE: ROBERT 'THE WOLFMAN' HOWARD

THE NEXT SEX ATTACKS

Now back in Ireland, and with a new name and a new job, Howard, or Cahill as he was calling himself could have gone on to lead a somewhat normal life. It seems though, that he was intent on sexual assault and rape as a preferred career choice and before long, he was up to his old tricks. In May of 1973, Howard broke into yet another house and tried to have his way with a woman of almost 60. The house was next door to the place he'd been staying and he must have done some reconnaissance on her situation as he knew she lived alone. He stole her belongings and beta her up, breaking her ankle as e dragged her around. Her tied her to the bed and repeatedly raped her before driving away in her car. She may have died if some family did not come for a visit the following morning.

Willie Doyle, a local police officer said of the attack:

"She was a very vulnerable person. She might have suffocated, but luckily for her some relations called the next morning and found her. She was very traumatised."

After a short investigation, police concluded that Howard was the perpetrator and a warrant was put out for his arrest. He was found at Dublin airport and the police noted how passive and courteous he seemed, far too polite to be the rapist villain they were looking for. Psychologists who interviewed Howard after the arrest stated that he should have been locked up for a very long time as he was an explosive and unpredictable psychopath. He could have been sentenced to life but instead he received 10 years imprisonment. This time there would be no release for good behaviour, although by all accounts it seems his second term in a HM Prison seems uneventful. He served the majority of his sentence and was released in 1981, where upon he returned to Wolfhill in Ireland and unsurprisingly continued on his life of criminality. This time there would be fatalities, quite how many is still not known to police.

MURDER FILE: ROBERT 'THE WOLFMAN' HOWARD

CONTINUED CRIMINALITY

Howard was mentioned in a report from a lady who had previous experience of sexual assault as the media found out about her appalling case of events. She was "the Kilkenny incest victim" and was repeatedly raped by her own sick father. He abused her, beat her, tortured and even impregnated her at the age of 15. She told police after the case emerged that Howard would come over to the house and drink whiskey with her father, sharing gruesome details of Howard's previous rapes and crimes and even boasting of new ones. After the story broke in the newspapers, the girl's father was arrested and sentenced to 7 years in prison. Thankfully, he would never be allowed to see his daughter again.

Somehow, Howard managed to find himself a wife and he married a young woman that he'd met in an Irish hospital. They married couple were awaiting social housing and drifted around the city of Dublin with no fixed abode for some time. Friends of the girl would have described her as vulnerable and deeply fragile, emotionally and physically, and they later told police that she'd told them just how evil and violently abusive Howard could be towards her. They lived a turbulent life together and drifted apart when he was jailed for robbery in 1988. He served another year and a half in prison, his 3rd spell, and travelled north of the border in 1990 to check himself into an alcohol addiction facility in Newry. After the treatment, which was run by nuns and given his personal experiences with the Catholic Church can't have been too successful, he met another woman called Pat Quinn and they moved together to Castlederg in County Tyrone. They registered for public housing but had a long line in front of them and ended up in a caravan site whilst they waited. It was during this wait that another young and vulnerable woman, aged just 22 was awaiting social housing and stayed for a few nights with Howard. According to her testimony, Howard tied her up and kept her prisoner for 3 weeks whilst repeatedly raping her. Family would eventually arrive to take her away but inevitably her life would never be the same after that awful experience. The worst part of this crime was that she got pregnant as a result of the rape but did not tell police until some years later and she was considered too weak to give evidence, and so Howard was never charged with this crime.

MURDER FILE: ROBERT 'THE WOLFMAN' HOWARD

PHSYCOLOGICAL PROFILING

When studied and questioned by specialists, Howard reacted very differently to what was expected. Judging from the growing list of awful crimes he had committed, psychologists expected a vile monster that was aggressive and arrogant when spoken to but he was far from that. He was smart and sophisticated, even charming when spoken to and he openly spoke of some of his crimes as though it were normal behaviour. Whether this came from his tormented life of institutions and homelessness remains to be seen but the life of crime he embarked upon sent him into a devastating spiral causing the emotional breakdown of many of his victims who were subjected to rape and vile abuse.

It was an extreme failure on the account of social services and of the authorities who failed to notice the actions and signs of a monster that was without remorse and preyed on vulnerable women of all ages and descriptions; even on children.

During sentencing for another rape charge, Dr Bownes, a psychiatrist working for the prosecution said:

"He has the propensity not only to commit further offences of a similar nature, but also to escalate his offending behaviour."

"He uses a sophisticated grooming process and selects vulnerable victims"

"Howard shows a pattern of behaviour had been established over many years and would be extremely resistant to change".

"I was somewhat surprised by the leniency of the sentence. In retrospect, we can see the system failed disastrously."

Dr Bownes was extremely concerned when the news broke about Howard's conviction and relatively short sentence of 3 years suspended sentence. Bownes had described Howard as a serial offender and if not locked away in an institution with the right facilities to treat his mental illness, he would undoubtedly reoffend and on an even larger scale.

MURDER FILE: ROBERT 'THE WOLFMAN' HOWARD

THE BEGINNING OF THE END

In January of 1995, Howard, who must have been quite used to this by now, was in court on a charge of rape. Quite astonishingly, even with the psychiatric reports available, Howard was given a 3 year suspended sentence and told to stay away from younger girls. Quite what sort of message this sent to the public is beyond comprehension but Howard was released and sent home. The judge must have hung his head in shame when he heard the news to come.

Upon release Howard was almost immediately in trouble again, this time not with the law but apparently with a splinter group of the IRA. Some high ranking members found out about Howard's activities and acted to put an end to it. Howard fled to Scotland, where he informed the housing association that he was being hunted and needed a secure residence. 2 months after his suspended sentence started, Glasgow council obliged and he started to live in a rough area of Glasgow, conveniently close to schools. Pat Quinn came and stayed with him whilst he moved for unknown reasons. The ground was shrinking beneath him as the PSNI, or Police Service of Northern Ireland had got their act together and informed Glasgow council about Howard's previous actions, or the criminal record that they knew of. This alone made him the prime suspect of the murder of Arlene Atkinson. He came back and forth from Ireland, but maintained permanent residence in Scotland, and Pat Quinn left him when he found a new, vulnerable girlfriend to prey on. He met the girl in a local pub and she had a 10 year old girl, who he may have also abused at some point.

The media then started to hound him. National papers started to publish pictures of his face and list in great detail his previous convictions and possible crimes. He was linked with almost every unsolved crime in the past 30 years and the public responded violently. A mob formed and gathered at his apartment, baying for blood. Howard escaped and was moved by the police to South London, where he was similarly hounded. He moved again to different locations and social services struggled to keep up with him. In 1999, a year before the millennium, a child protection officer noted that he was living in Kent with a woman called Mary.

MURDER FILE: ROBERT 'THE WOLFMAN' HOWARD

THE END OF THE ROAD

Hannah Williams had lived an unfortunate childhood. Her parents had bitterly gone their separate ways and she herself had been subject to sexual abuse from her mother's boyfriend. She had been admitted to facilities that deal with these issues and they noted she had learning difficulties and behavioural issues. In 2001 she was living in a rundown area of Deptford, South London.

The worst possible thing then happened as she was introduced to Howard, through his girlfriend Mary as Hannah and Mary knew each other well through Hannah's mother. Howard apparently took great interest in her and the mother and Mary must have not known about Howard's past because they cannot have understood what would happen next. Hannah took a little trip to the market, alone, and met her brother who was working there. Deptford was not a particularly prosperous area and she had very little money but she dreamed of buying new clothes and shoes. Kevin, her brother remembered hearing her take a phone call and she said "I'm going now."

Hannah had never run away from home, despite her previous troubles, and her mother started to worry when she didn't come home. She had told her mother previously that she was going to meet a friend but she would never come home from wherever she was. She frantically called the police and they didn't seem to take the report seriously so Bernadette went looking on her own. She recruited friends and fellow community members who would work in shifts, driving around the streets looking for the young girl. She made posters and phoned everybody she possibly could to get any information regarding her whereabouts. Several police officers were dismissed after the investigation for not taking enough care and due diligence in the initial stages of the investigation, and with good reason. The media published her pictures and launched campaigns but she was not found and her mother was understandably heartbroken. Her body would not be found for another year.

Workers were clearing a piece of land to make way for a new flyover as part of the Channel Tunnel development when they uncovered something in the undergrowth. Almost a year after the disappearance, a machine used for clearing large pieces of dirt uncovered the decomposing body of a young girl. She had been wrapped in blue plastic and police initially thought it had been another missing girl until the matched the clothes to those Hannah had been wearing on the day she went missing. Police informed Bernadette of the discovery, but she had already seen what was going on via the news on television and she was distraught.

"I finally found out my daughter was dead, and that her body had been found, by watching it on the telly. To find out that way was unforgivable. I screamed and then I cried and cried."

"She would have made a beautiful bride, but instead of a white wedding, we had a white funeral."

Police examined the decomposing remains and did not take long to draw a list of suspects. Top of the list was Robert

Howard and the giveaway had been that he'd used his girlfriend Mary's mobile phone to call her just before she died. She'd been raped and strangled in the most horrific way and the rope was still around the neck of the body when it was found. Howard was arrested in March 2002 and would not leave prison for the remainder of his life.

The trial was set for the following year and although they had no forensic evidence of Howard's involvement, they had circumstantial evidence as his whereabouts could not be proven at the time of her disappearance and the long line of character witnesses that wanted to put Howard away for the rest of his life. A young girl even came to court to tell the judge that Howard had tried to take her to exactly the same place where the murder had happened and assault her but she'd escaped.

Gradually, victims from the past bravely came forward and gave grizzly details from their ordeals at the man who called himself The Wolfman. Previous victims told of the particular methods that Howard used in his attacks, namely with the rope around the neck which happened to be the link they needed. In 3 short hours, the jury finished their verdict and were obviously sickened by the offences Howard had committed as they gave a guilty verdict and sent him for sentencing.

MURDER FILE: ROBERT 'THE WOLFMAN' HOWARD

SENTENCING

The judge delivered a damning verdict of the authorities who'd let him go with lenient sentences in the past and held nothing back when delivering his verdict. Mr Justice McKinnon, the judge presiding over the case said that he had no regrets about handing Howard a life sentence and that he only wished it had been done sooner.

"It is clear that you are a danger to teenage girls and other women, and have been for a very long time."

Howard, though now serving a life sentence was also still under investigation for the murder of Arlene Atkinson, and the media were restricted on what they could publish. When the verdict of life was given, the families rejoiced as they felt they could finally start to grieve as the monster had been put away for the rest of his life. Surprisingly, Howard was acquitted of the murder of Arlene in Belfast because previous evidence could not be introduced into the court. There was a furious uproar from the public who noted the flaws of the legal system and felt Arlene deserved more justice than that. In the United States, Howard would have faced the death penalty. The jury were aware of the criminal history of Robert Howard but they were not allowed to use this as evidence.

Since the sentencing and whilst in prison, Howard cut a lonely figure and psychologists tried to study his behaviour. It seemed as though he was resigned to spending his remaining days in relative peace behind the prison walls and he kept to himself whilst the media tried to pin every crime in the unsolved case book on him. It would not surprise many to find him guilty of at least a few of those crimes and a taskforce was set up amongst investigators collaborating from Northern Ireland, Ireland and the United Kingdom. Inquiries were also set up to deal with the handling of Howard and his early releases for which there was still no explanation. He was allowed freedom when he should have had none for the earlier crimes he committed and the public were rightfully outraged.

MURDER FILE: ROBERT 'THE WOLFMAN' HOWARD

AFTERMATH

Robert Howard was the subject of much debate and media attention after the full details of his brutal past came to light. The spotlight shined on the legal system and specifically dealings and failures made between deals between the governments of the United Kingdom and Ireland. These failures let a clearly psychotic rapist loose, and allowed him to murder one girl, probably 2 and possible more.

A journalist wrote a book about missing Women from Ireland and has linked Howard to many disappearances over the periods of time he was out of jail. He stressed the importance of further investigations,

"This was a man who travelled freely all over Ireland and the UK, and lived in many places. The police should be looking at all unsolved disappearances, murders and sex crimes against women and girls during the periods when he was at large. They should be asking, 'Where was Howard?' "

As a direct result of Robert Howard, Ireland set up a sexual offenders register in 2001, many years after it should have and liaison between the police forces of all nations involved have improved when it comes to searching for dangerous suspects. The monitoring of sex offenders' on the lists in all nations involved has also improved and anonymous phone lines have been set up for victims of any sexual attacks.

The family of Hannah got closure after the trial and they would not have been sad to hear the news of his passing. His death, although he suffered in jail for some time, would have been bittersweet as young Hannah would have grown into a beautiful woman but she now would never have the opportunity. It was equally sad for the parents of Arlene Atkinson, whose parents knew the killer of their daughter, but he was never punished for the crime.

MURDER FILE: ROBERT 'THE WOLFMAN' HOWARD

SUMMARY

Robert 'The Wolfman' Howard was a sick and twisted killer. He was also a skilled one that targeted vulnerable children and meticulously and ruthlessly preyed upon them. He groomed girls into thinking he was a safe person to be with and he played the system. He tracked down marginalised, vulnerable women to use as cover and seduced them into thinking he was harmless.

From a young age Howard was failed by the system. At first he was failed by the Catholic institutions for young offenders where he was beaten, starved and manipulated beyond comprehension. Only recently have these institutions been found out and closed down for good. He was also failed by his family during childhood, where he was thrown out and forced to fend for himself. The troubles in the institutions, followed by the awful upbringing and living rough meant he was not of a sound mind from an early age and the failures continued.

He was failed by the justice system of both Ireland and the UK, who failed to spot the risks he posed to the public and he was not given the correct rehabilitation and support as his crimes grew in violence and stature. In this respect the public were also failed as the justice system did not protect the scores of victims from the evil man. It was quite clear from reading the long list of crimes he committed, even before he murdered that he should not have been allowed to roam the streets as he stole and raped his way through 4 different countries. The security forces of these countries failed to keep tabs on him and monitor his life of crime.

So the life of the Wolfman would appear to be a life full of failures. He was clearly psychotic and possibly schizophrenic given the reaction of the Irish police force when the arrested him and said he seemed like a nice man. He was indeed a charming fellow, but also a brutal murderer that preyed on children and women and had a brutal past. He was of no use to anyone. Perhaps the only good thing to come from researching about this person is the fact that Ireland set up a sex offenders' list, practically as a result of his actions and support for victims of this crime grew. Liaison between police forces also developed to catch future sex attackers that try to evade the law by moving around. It does not make for good reading, researching the life of this person and not a nice a word has been mentioned about him. I feel deep sympathy for the victims' families and to the victims of his ruthless sex attacks. His was a life dedicated to crime and it was allowed to continue for a great deal longer than it should have. Let us hope that the lessons have been learned on all sides of this story and someone like Robert Howard is never allowed to do anything similar ever again.

A MONSTER IN THE CHURCH

PAULA HEARST

CHAPTER ONE

It was a cold winter night in November when the Hansen family attended a service at the Jehovah Lutheran Church in St.Paul, Minnesota. It was a "family night" at the church. Ellen Hansen and her two daughters, Cassie and Vanessa had looked forward to the evening at the church. There would be interactive games and stories plus the young girls would be able to see their friends.

Bill, the girl's father, had other business to attend to that night. He watched as his young daughters got into the car with his wife.

"It is etched in my memory," Bill Hansen recalled. "We had supper and the girls got in the car. Ellen was driving. And they were in the garage and Cassie was sitting in the passenger seat. And she (Cassie) was blowing kisses at me through the window. Waving goodbye."

Ellen arrived at the church at around 6:40 p.m for the 7:00 service. They liked to arrive early and socialize with the other church members before the sermon began. The girls proceeded to go to the children's area, located on the lower level of the church. It was their designated place to be as they usually had their Sunday School classes there, they called it the "Kid's Kingdom."

"I have to go to the bathroom," Cassie said to her mother at around 6:50 p.m.

"Okay," Ellen said. "You know where it's at?"

"I'll be right back," Cassie nodded her head.

Ellen watched her daughter leave and returned her attention to Vanessa and her other playmates. A few minutes later, however, Ellen realized that Cassie had not returned to the auditorium area and began to search for her daughter.

"Cassie?" Ellen called out.

She passed the rest of congregants milling into the auditorium. Her eyes scanning for her daughter among the clusters of families filing into the church.

"Cassie!"

"What's wrong?" one of the church staff members asked.

"I can't find my daughter," Ellen said.

The two began searching for the little girl, poking their head in the bathroom stalls and then going through every nook and cranny of the church.

"She's wearing a blue dress," Ellen said, trying to collect her thoughts. "She's blonde. Blue dress. Blue skirt. White blouse.

It started as a casual search. Cassie had probably went somewhere inside the church, got distracted and lost track of time.

"There you are!" would be the words everyone expected to hear.

As the minutes went by, however, this casual search soon turned into full blown panic. All of the staff members and congregants now began searching through the church, going upstairs and down.

"Cassie!"

Her heart pounding out of her chest, Ellen called her husband.

"I got the phone call from Ellen," Bill said. "Saying that Cassie was missing. And my heart stopped and I think I was breathing heavy, you know, just thinking 'oh boy,' because you know your child and you know that she would just not walk away from something like that. Right away, I know something was definitely wrong."

Ellen and the congregation looked throughout the church for Cassie to no avail.

The police arrived and the response was immediate. Cassie's photograph was promptly distributed to every news outlet and street flyers were made on the spot.

The search began and lasted all night.

"We stayed up all night," Ellen said. "People came all night long to help. There were a couple hundred people. Helping us search."

Police did door to door search in the neighborhood, inquiring with folks with a picture of Cassie. Church and neighborhood volunteers rallied right away and a command center was set up at the church.

There was no sign of Cassie.

She had disappeared into thin air.

CHAPTER TWO

The next morning at 11 o'clock, the police found Cassie's body

"Oh no!" one of the congregants screamed as the word was given to the people who had gathered in the church.

"The search has been called off," the officer in charge said solemnly.

In a dumpster, behind an auto repair shop that was three miles from the church, the body of Cassie Hansen had been found.

The members of the church wailed in agony. Some people stood in shock, frozen in grief.

Things like this don't happen here.

"It truly incensed the community," one of the officers on the scene said. "It incensed a lot of police officers. It was as if he seemed to be treating her as a piece of trash."

One of Cassie's leather shoes without the buckles were found a few blocks away from the dumpster while her second shoe was found later nearby.

"The idea of a church is one place you can go and you'd let your daughter go to a restroom," Catherine Lowe, crime reporter said. "That's something you would do. You'd feel a safeness, there are good people all in there together the last thing you would ever expect, and you'd have no reason to expect a stranger to come into a church and abduct a child."

The autopsy on Cassie's body would reveal no sexual penetration but that some type of sexual act had taken place.

Semen found on her dress would reveal that the perpetrator had type O blood. They would also find unusual, foreign hairs.

Cassie had been strangled to death by a two and a half inch belt, the time of death occurring between 8 o'clock and midnight. The young girl had abrasions on her body which indicated that another belt was used to restrain her. The child had been punched in her face, head, ribs and shoulder. She had scratches on her face that were consistent with someone's hand being held over her mouth.

The police did have one vague description of a possible suspect, however.

One of the church congregants reported seeing a Caucasian male, about 50-60 years old, enter the bathroom area on the night of Cassie's disappearance. He had white hair and glasses.

Who was he?

Police went to work, digging up information on any and all sex offenders in the area.

"We had a total of 107 people who had been identified by the community," an officer said. "Or through police investigation of being possible suspects. Of those 107 individuals, 57 of them either lived or worked in the area where the little girl was abducted from."

Police would rounded up these past offenders and the interrogations began.

They quickly got a suspect and then a confession.

From a crazy woman.

"Vondell Quanley," Thomas Poch said. "A woman from Texas who had claimed to have killed Cassie Hansen. And when she came to the attention of St. Paul police and allegedly made a confession it turned out that what she did was read details in the paper and then recite them. She said 'I claim I acted alone.' Well, it was quite obvious that she couldn't generate seminal fluid and that this was a sham and a fraud."

A helpful call did come in, however. Two witnesses claim that they saw an older white male carrying a motionless child near the auto body shop dumpster on the night Cassie disappeared.

Police followed up on this lead as it echoed what the church congregant witnessed near the church bathrooms.

An elderly white man. White hair. Glasses.

Needing more to go on, the St. Paul police contacted the FBI unit.

With their assistance, the FBI helped St. Paul police come up with a behavioral profile of the child murderer.

"The killer is most likely a Caucasian male," the FBI profiler said. "Someone who is considered a loner."

"How do you mean?"

"We're not talking about someone who is the life of the party here. He can blend in. He can be invisible."

"So the people in church wouldn't necessarily notice him right off the bat?"

"Precisely," the profiler said. "This is a guy who doesn't think a whole lot of himself and automatically thinks that everyone around him sees him the same way. No value. So he keeps to himself and lashes out when he can. He probably has a low-level job or is unemployed. Probably has had numerous sex offenses in the past. He likes to frequent parks or schoolyards. You know, the creepy guy standing on the periphery. He's a voyeur. He watches his victims from afar before making his move. He trolls around at night, thinking of himself as some kind of predator. He can hide better at night. It brings out his mood, his compulsion."

"Do you think he's still here?"

"That's the illogical thing. The perp will not leave the area. He is limited in funds and can't move around easy. He feels put upon and justified in his actions. That he's entitled to whatever he wants. So he often takes a souvenir from his victims. A lock of hair. An article of clothing. Anything that marks the moment. His moment of triumph. He may also return to the scene of the crime, feeling the need to talk about it with someone."

CHAPTER THREE

The perp in the case of Cassie Hansen, did just that courtesy of Dorothy Noga.

Noga, a masseuse at the Comfort Center in St. Paul, called in a tip for the police when she became suspicious of one of her clients.

One of her customers, a cab driver named Stuart Knowlton, had been in her massage parlor the day after Cassie's murder.

Noga remembered Knowlton coming into her parlor at 3 a.m in the morning to introduce himself to the staff. He was hunched over, breathing heavy and talked really fast as if he had just been in a sprint.

He handed out business cards to everyone and received a massage from Noga.

"How's that feel?" Noga asked as she kneaded Knowlton's back.

"Great," Stuart said. "But I need a favor."

"What's that?" Noga asked, expecting the usual request for a "special" massage.

"If anyone asks, tell them I was in here last night."

That made Noga suspicious, knowing that Cassie had been murdered the night before.

Stuart Knowlton looked suspicious and fit the profile. He was Caucasian and 56 years old. Single, he worked a low-level job as a taxi driver. He had beady blue eyes set behind thick-set glasses.

Eyes that gave off the thousand yard stare that only a true psychopath can pull off.

He 'looked' the part. But was he the guy?

"I have no urge for any little girls," Knowlton said during police questioning. "I feel sorry for the little girl for her family. But I did not kill her. I didn't even know she was missing until.."

"Is it possible you killed her and forgot?"

"No sir," Knowlton said. "I did not kill her."

"Where were you on the night of the murder?"

"I was on duty driving my taxi cab. Could not have been me."

Noga followed up with police and offered to tape record her conversations with Knowlton.

Police, however, declined her offer as it would have been too dangerous for the masseuse.

The police also did not want to be seen as obtaining information illegally after Knowlton had contacted a lawyer and the lawyer had told him not to talk. Noga decided to override the police order, however. She was a good listener and could always get men to open up to her. She had four kids of her own and wanted to make the safe streets for other families.

She would then have daily phone conversations with Knowlton with same lasting deep into the night. She described him as being "lonely" and that he could not stop talking about Cassie Hansen's murder.

Noga knew that he was the man who did it.

On one occasion, Noga had taken Knowlton out for a drive. They drove past Cassie's church and noticed that Knowlton had become very agitated and wanted to leave.

The nightly phone calls soon became very taxing. Knowlton believed that the two had some kind of romantic connection. Noga was soon putting herself into a corner that she couldn't escape from.

"I would get so depressed talking to him," Noga told the St. Paul Dispatch. "I wanted to give up. I would just sit and cry."

But finally he broke.

Stuart Knowlton confessed to killing Cassie Hansen.

Noga then started taping their conversations and gave the police the tapes. The police encouraged her to keep up the conversations but Knowlton never mentioned his involvement with the murder again. He still talked about the case in a roundabout way but never confessed to the killing again.

The police would catch another break in the case as another person familiar with Knowlton came forward.

Her name was Janice Rettman. She was in charge of St. Paul's Public Housing Office and met Knowlton when he complained that he was about to be evicted from a Roosevelt Homes public housing project. He stated that his wife was leaving him and taking their two children. The welfare payments and food stamps they had been cut off and he had just begun driving a cab. Rettman investigated his claims, however, and discovered that those were not the reasons he was being evicted.

Residents had complained made sexual advances toward young girls in the housing unit.

Knowlton had let two fourteen year old girls into his apartment to play cards. Once inside, he began describing to them where babies came from and began talking about sex, birth control and menstruation. He then asked if they wanted to see his penis. The girls reported the incident to police which then informed the public housing office. Knowlton was then given a warning by the office that if such an incident would occur again he would be evicted.

Knowlton wouldn't heed the warning. He confronted a nine year old girl and told her to take her pants off for him. The girl was so traumatized that she had recurring nightmares of Knowlton.

Knowlton's wife and children were taken to a women's shelter while he lived in an efficiency apartment. He then told Rettman of his sexual preference for children. He revealed he had spent time in a mental hospital in Traverse City, Michigan after he molested a seven year old girl. He alleged that his own father routinely beat and abused him. And he would talk about shoes a lot.

"I can't remember anyone being as chilling as he was," Rettman recalled as she knew that Knowlton frequented the area where Cassie was murdered. As a cab driver, he would be familiar with the ins and outs of the streets there, the back streets and alleys.

She would call to double-check on his housing situation and found him upset and unwilling to talk. He hung up on her but called her back a few days later. Knowlton said that he "was going through hell, was very lonely, and needed someone to talk to and to visit him."

Rettman offered her services to police, stating that she could meet with Knowlton and wear a wire.

Police accepted her offer.

Knowlton would tell Rettman about the child molestation charges from the Roosevelt Homes, his problems with his wife and his inability to hold down a job. He talked about how he converted to Christianity the previous year after being inspired by a Johnny Cash song.

Knowlton would also make reference to his "explosive temper" during their conversation and mistakenly call Rettman "Dorothy" on two occasions.

"Have you been following the news about Cassie Hansen?" Rettman asked.

"Yeah, I have," Knowlton said. "Police came and talked to me about it."

"Really?"

"They want to find out if he and I were together. If he were up there at the time of the Hansen's girls beatings. I don't even remember where I was that night."

The police then knew they had incriminating evidence against Knowlton. The fact that Cassie had been beaten up had not been released to the public.

"That was crucial and that was very critical," Thomas Poch, prosecuting attorney said. "Because no one had revealed to the press, to the media, to anyone, that she'd been beaten. And only the killer could have known that.

Meanwhile, we didn't have any witnesses. It was entirely a circumstantial case."

CHAPTER FOUR

Police followed through with Knowlton's claim that he was working on the night that Cassie Hansen was murdered. With the cooperation of the taxi company, they realized that Knowlton had not turned in his log book. The log book was the time and location of all of a taxi driver's pick-ups and drop-offs.

"What happened to your log book?" police asked Knowlton in another interview.

"It was stolen," Knowlton said.

Knowlton's dispatcher, Donald Whalen would state that he tried to radio Knowlton several times during the night of Cassie's disappearance and could not reach him. Knowlton then tried to buy blank trip sheets from a competing cab company on the day Cassie's body was found.

Dorothy Noga decided to ignore police warnings that Knowlton was dangerous. With her poofy brown hair and overly applied black eye-liner, Noga did not fit the profile of a police informant. She did, however, prove to answer the hero's call when needed.

Noga called Knowlton again in the hopes of entrapping him into making incriminating statements.

"So have you been following the news about Cassie?" Noga asked. "The little girl that was murdered."

"She was a hero for us," one of the police officers said. "She told us that during one of these conversations that he admitted to her that he had killed the little girl. That he had, in effect, killed Cassie. Dorothy Noga agreed and wanted to help in the case and stated that she would be willing to talk to him and to tape these conversations. And she did this hours on end."

Knowlton, however, would not repeat what he told Noga on the phone during their earlier conversation.

Noga didn't realize how much danger she had exposed herself to. After getting off the phone with Knowlton, she was about to close her massage parlor that evening and was confronted by a man inside.

The attack was swift. She left up her hands in defense but the knife slashed through. She squirmed to get away but her assailant stabbed her in the back then slashed down her throat.

Noga crumpled to the ground, losing consciousness as she bled out.

Her assailant escaped into the darkness, blood dripping from his knife.

The thirty-two year old Noga was discovered in the parlor and rushed to the hospital.

"I proceeded to the hospital," one of the policemen on duty said. "Her throat had been slit. Her blood pressure was down to zero. They were certain she was going to die."

Noga would recover from her attack, however. She had been slashed in her throat, back and wrist right after she attempted to record Knowlton's confession.

But Noga had no recollection of the attack. She had to be placed under hypnosis in order to remember the specific details.

During hypnosis, Dorothy was able to remember who stabbed her that night.

She remembered the man's face in the darkness.

It was Stuart Knowlton.

"He jammed a knife straight on in my neck," Noga recalled in a television interview. "Then he pulled it out. Then I knew that he had cut me and I turned my head and he said 'I'll teach you not to talk' and he cut it and he slit it (her throat) all the way down."

She remembered that Stuart had confronted her and accused her of going to the police. He then confessed to the crime, giving her all of the specific details. After he confessed, he took out a knife and began chasing her around the sauna until he slashed at her throat and she lost consciousness.

CHAPTER FIVE

Minnesota State law permits testimony obtained from hypnosis, so any testimony from Noga would have been deemed inadmissible.

The police then focused on the science of the crime.

They had a semen sample that was Type O. DNA was still a long way away from acceptance back in the early 1980s but Stuart Knowlton had Type O blood. The police then acquired a hair sample from Knowlton, sending that along with Cassie Hansen's clothing to the FBI forensic laboratory.

The techs then scraped off any loose hairs and fibers from Cassie's clothing. They wanted to match Knowlton's hair sample with anything on Cassie's clothing.

"Hair comparisons are not a means of absolute personal identification," FBI Lab expert Al Robillard said. "Because a hair matches an individual or has the same microscopic characteristics as that individual's hairs, does not absolutely mean that it came from him. The reason for that is hairs are not so unique that they allow you to reach an absolute conclusion. Its possible that two hairs are so alike that they can't be distinguished microscopically could come from two separate individuals."

But Robillard would make a hair discovery on Cassie's dress that he had never seen before.

"What's so unusual in my career, looking at hairs at the FBI laboratory, I have never seen or I have never matched a hair that had this unusual characteristic. A hair disease called pili annulati. Commonly that is referred to as either ringed hair or banded hair. So I thought this was rather significant."

"If you think of looking at a racoon's tail, you actually see bands. And these bands are created because there is a breakdown in that area of the cuticle that begins to separate."

Robillard then took samples of Knowlton's hair and matched from the ones on Cassie's dress. They both had the same condition.

Pili annulati.

"No doubt about it," Robillard said looking back. "Thousands of hairs over the course of my career. I was only to put two hairs, associate a victim to a suspect, not only through the microscopic characteristics but also through a disease of the hair."

The hair was enough to arrest Knowlton for Cassie's murder.

But asthe police were closing in on Knowlton, the taxi cab driver suffered an accident.

He was crossing the street in St. Paul when a motorist ran into him. The suspect was transported to the hospital where surgeons had to amputate his left leg below the knee.

"It just seemed to me that divine intervention was there," one of the police officers said. "And that the children were going to be protected and that he would not be able to grab another child."

CHAPTER SIX

Noga would take the stand during Knowlton's trial and tell jurors of the telephone call before he attacked her.

"He said he was driving his taxi cab in the vicinity of the Jehovah Evangelical Lutheran church when he needed to use the bathroom," Noga said. "It was there I saw Cassie Hansen."

Knowlton then described greeting Cassie outside the bathroom, talking to her about the church services.

"Would you like to play a game?" he asked.

The girl nodded but remained unsure.

Knowlton lured her outside. Cassie began to cry.

He then her into his cab and molested her.

The little girl kept crying so he put his hand over her mouth until she stopped breathing.

He would then take off both of her shoes before placing her into the dumpster. Knowlton had removed the buckle from the shoe and kept it as a souvenir before dumping the shoes in two separate locations.

"Stuart had a shoe fetish," Janice Rettman said. "When he talked about shoes at first, it meant nothing to me. In retrospect, it was probably more significant than I thought."

The unique hair found on Cassie's hair clothing that matched Stuart Knowlton's own hair strand was enough to convince the jury to find him guilty of first degree murder and second degree misconduct.

He was sentenced to life in prison.

"The evidence from the FBI laboratory was absolutely critical and one piece of evidence that was absolutely essential to tying him in and being able to get a conviction of Stuart Knowlton."

Knowlton was given an opportunity to speak after his sentencing and he went on an incoherent ten minute rant.

"As God is my witness," Knowlton rambled on "I swear to you this day, I did not abduct Cassandra Lynn Hansen from the church she was attending. I had no reason to take anyone's life for God had not given me that right. I have had no reason to have any vengeance against Cassandra Lynn Hansen or Dorothy Noga."

Knowlton would die in prison in 2006 after being denied parole in 2001.

After his sentencing, the Hansen family started a foundation called "Save Cassie's Friends." Two hundred books were printed out in Cassie's honor, raising awareness of child abduction.

Football Player & Serial Killer : The True Story of Randall Woodfield

Sarah Teague

On October 9th, 1980, Portland, Oregon police arrived at grime scene. A pretty young woman with soft facial features and dark brown, shoulder-length hair was found dead. She suffered from repeated stab wounds in her neck, as well as evidence of blunt force trauma, as if from a severe bludgeoning. The victim was Cherie Ayers, a twenty-nine year old woman who was found dead in her home. She was the first of a trail of bodies scattered throughout Oregon. From October 1980 to the blistery winter of February 1981, a span of grisly murders would plague the rainy pacific northwest state of Oregon up and down the I-5 - or, the Highway of Hell. The culprit was dubbed "The I-5 Killer", leaving behind at least ten known victims. The identity of the killer turned out to be former 17th round draft pick for the Green Bay Packers, Randall Woodfield.

Randall Woodfield would be convicted of only one of his heinous murders by the summer of 1981, though Woodfield has been tried to at least eighteen victims up and town Interstate 5. Woodfield spent the two years between 1979 and 1981 terrorizing the citizens of Oregon and Washington, a time of horror that lives on in the memories of those that witnessed and lived through it. Woodfield was not born and raised in typical, serial killer fashion. There are no horrors in his past, nor is there a trail of neglect leading back to his childhood. The story of Randall Woodfield turning from Green Bay Packers prospect to serial killer is one that doesn't have a logical explanation.

Just after Christmas Day in December of 1950, Randall Brent Woodfield was born. Woodfield was born into a middle class family in the town of Salem, Oregon. His childhood and homelife were, overall, normal. His family had no dysfunctional habits to speak of. He was the only son of a stay at home mother and a father who worked as the executive of Pacific Northwest Bell, a phone company. Woodfield was his parent's only boy, and no doubt luxuriated in such a fact. He had two older sisters, one of whom worked as a doctor and the other as a lawyer. He grew up middle class with what one would assume would be a fairly comfortable life. The Woodfield family was well-known throughout their community, and had no prior issues with deviant behavior or dysfunction. Growing up, he was a popular kid among the rest of his high school classmates. As well as socially, Woodfield excelled academically. He got good grades, and the teachers had no reason to be concerned with his performance.

It was in highschool that he his natural skills in regards to football were discovered. His parents encouraged him to pursue athletics. With enough talent, Woodfield was the start player of the football team that he played for at Newport High School. Despite his otherwise normal upbringing, and Woodfield's likeability among his peers, teachers and coaches, problems began to arise for Woodfield beginning in his adolescence. He began exposing himself and engaging in otherwise sexually charged antisocial behavior. He got caught exposing himself to women and girls while standing on a bridge. That was his first offense in a long line of criminal behavior that would turn out to shock the entirety of the Pacific Northwest.

There was no outcry from his teachers or coaches, however. Woodfield was referred, by his parents, to a therapist to talk about the issue. The therapist didn't find any cause for concern, and said that Woodfield was simply a teenager exploring his newfound sexuality. There was such little worry over the incident that Woodfield's coaches managed to get him out of his first arrest during high school, in regards to indecent exposure, so that he could continue his role on the football team. At eighteen, his record was expunged and the first signs of deviant behavior were erased, but for the memories that live on in those that had witnessed it.

Woodfield lived a mostly normal and undisruptive childhood and adolescence. At the least, there was nothing to suggest the dangerous and dark path he would soon head down that would lead police slogging through victims up and down the I-5 through Oregon and Washington. From Newport High School's team, Woodfield went on to Portland State University, where he continued to play football - and where his behavior continued to take a turn for the worst. Despite this, many people had only good things to say about Woodfield.

Woodfield was recalled differently between both his teammates and his coaches at Portland State University. Gary Hamblet, who worked as a PSU receivers coach during the time that Woodfield attended college there, recalls him to have been "the nicest, most gentlemanly kid" he ever knew. On the other hand, a former PSU teammate said this of Woodfield: "You just had a bad feeling about the guy, like there was something underneath his mask."

Woodfield, despite playing on the football team, was hesitant to allow himself any physical contact with the other players. He was incredibly fast, and his coaches remarked on his speed that made him a valuable player. It was just that Woodfield had an aversion to allowing himself to be hit by anyone else on either his own or the opposing the team.

This aversion was just part of Woodfields general personality. He was soft spoken and would avoid confrontation, which made him well liked by teachers and coaches. Woodfield was also considered quite handsome, standing at six feet and muscular, with dark hair and a distinguished mustache that wouldn't be out of place for a college-aged guy in the 70s. His general attractive demeanor made him just as likeable as his personality.

Woodfield took part in the Campus Crusade for Christ, as well as the Fellowship of Christian Athletes. He was well known for both of these activities, and his teammates recall them being a very important part of his life at Portland State University. Woodfield would have been considered a "good guy", as demonstrated by his devotion to the on-campus Christian organizations. This gentle demeanor, however, was at severe odds with the criminal and antisocial behavior that Woodfield often demonstrated. Woodfield was 20 years old when, in 1970, he was arrested for the vandalization of an ex-girlfriend's apartment in Ontario, Oregon while he was attending a community college before his eventual transfer to Portland State University. He was arrested twice more that year for displays of public indecency. The amicable quality about him that Woodfield had demonstrated during his time at Newport High School didn't seem to follow him to PSU.

Woodfield's teammates had a mixed bag of feelings towards him. He was described by one of his teammates, Jon Carey, as "confident in himself, but not to the point of being cocky". He wasn't a loner by any means, and had a relatively normal dating history. Despite this, some of Woodfield's other teammates remember him being a little strange. According to some, Woodfield was prone to making statements that seemed apropos of nothing, with his line of thinking hard to follow.

While he was attending PSU, Woodfield was being watched by scouts for the Green Bay Packers. Strangely enough, no one thought to run any sort of background check. In the 17th round of the NHL draft picks that year in 1974, Green Bay drafted Randall Woodfield, unknowing of both his previous foray into antisocial sexual behaviors or the arrests on his record for indecent exposure and vandalism. Perhaps, had they known, the Packers would not have continued on with Woodfield on their team. Woodfield did not hesitate once offered the contract. He was on the edge of making it big, having been signed to play in the NFL. He was given a $16,000 one-year contract with thousands of dollars in bonuses if he played well.

However, Woodfield stay with Green Bay would be short lived. He attended a training camp during April of 1974 located in Scottsdale, Arizona. He was assessed by the coaches and seemed to have high hopes of cutting it on the team. In July, Woodfield competed in a game against the Bears which turned out as well as expected. Woodfield continued to make several cuts, and was otherwise looking forward to staying on with the Packers and the NFL. In August of 1974, however, Woodfield was abruptly cut from the team. He stayed in Wisconsin after this, and played for the Manitowoc Chiefs in hopes that the

Packers would change their mind and welcome him back onto the team.

Woodfield played well, and got along with his teammates in Manitowoc. He continued having a relatively well-rounded life, with teammates, friends and girlfriends. After his first season with Manitowoc, though, Woodfield was let go from that team as well. It was shortly after his release from the Chiefs that Woodfield drove back to his home state of Oregon. It was that year in 1975 that Woodfield escalated from petty vandalism and indecent exposure to crimes that would become more and more horrific as time went on.

Woodfield's crime spree began in the early months of 1975. In Portland, a string of women were being held at knife-point by a man who would then rape them or force them to perform sexual acts on him. The man would then rob them of their handbags, though murder did not seem to be on the agenda for this particular assailant. Portland police used female police officers as undercover decoys to catch the perpetrator, and used marked dollar bills to track down the man. As it turns out, it was Randall Woodfield. In early March, Woodfield was arrested after trying to rob the undercover female officers. In April that same year, Woodfield plead guilty to second-degree robbery. He was originally sentenced for ten years in prison, but managed to get out on parole in July of 1979.

There's no way to tell what happened in those four years that Woodfield spent in prison. There is also no way to tell if he had served out his full span of ten years, whether or not he would have eventually escalated his crimes the way that he did. All that is know, is that after his released from prison in July of 1979, Woodfield began his reign of terror enacted along the I-5 that lends him his nickname, the I-5 Killer.

Woodfield's first known victim was 29 year old Cherie Ayers, though there's no way to tell if Woodfield was simply not able to be connected with any previous murders before October 8th in 1980. Ayers was one of Woodfield's former classmates at Newport High

School. They knew one another casually, socially, after they had reconnected at their high school reunion. She was found dead in her apartment in Portland. She was beaten to death and stabbed in her throat. There was also evidence of sexual assault to her body. Woodfield was picked up for this crime before his spree of killings along the I-5 began. Unfortunately, police were unable to link him to Cherie Ayers, neither by blood test nor semen found on the body. Ultimately, Woodfield was released, despite the police finding him "evasive" when asking questions regarding his possible involvement with the crime.

There's no telling what evading the police made Woodfield feel, or whether or not that incident made him confident enough to continue on with his future murders. On thanksgiving morning, not one month later from Cherie Ayer's death, 22 year old Darcey Renee Fix and 24 year old Douglas Keith Altig were found shot, execution style, in Fix's home in Northern Portland. The gun used was a .32 revolver belonging to fix, which was missing from the crime scene. Sure enough, Woodfield was not a stranger to these two victims, either. Darcey Fix was the ex-girlfriend of one of his former PSU teammates. Police picked up Woodfield a second time, and a second time they were unable to tie Woodfield definitely to the crime.

Throughout December of 1980, Portland was once more plagued with a series of robberies at both knifepoint and gun-point. The assailant as described to be wearing a fake beard and a strip of white athletic tape over his nose, like the kind an athlete would wear. Or, more specifically, the manner in which a football player might wear it. The crimes ranged from armed robbery of a gas station in Vancouver, Washington to forcing a twenty-five year old waitress to masurbate him at gunpoint in the bathroom of a diner. All of these crimes were taking place up and down Interstate 5 that runs up and down alongside the pacific coast between Canada and Mexico. The crimes, however, were isolated to Oregon and Washington, and all happened within two miles of the I-5. This is what lead police to give him the moniker: The

I-5 Bandit, which would later become the I-5 Killer after Woodfield stint with robbery was up and he, once more, turned to murder.

The armed robberies continued on as December turned into a blistery and rainy January of 1981. Throughout January, Woodfield—who was still evading the police, and who was now only known by law enforcement as the I-5 Bandit—would go back and rob the same exact Vancouver gas station, then move on to perform another armed robbery on a market in Eugene. By January 12th, he was in Sutherlin, Oregon, where he wounded a female grocery clerk by gunshot during a robbery of the store. Nowhere was safe. The I-5 Bandit was moving quickly between towns up and down Interstate 5, slipping from Washington to Oregon and leaving no trace of himself behind at his crime scenes.

The crimes kept escalating, going from robbery and sexual assault to pedophilia. On January 14th, Woodfield, wearing his fake beard, committed a home invasion where two young girls lived. They were ages eight and ten. Woodfield force the young children to take off their clothes, then proceeded to sexually assault them. It was only four days later that Woodfield, have returned to his hometown of Salem, Oregon, entered an office building where he once more committed sexual violence against two women by the names of Shari Hull and Lisa Garcia. It was here that Woodfield's life of crime escalated from robbery and rape, once more to murder. Woodfield shot both Hull and Garcia. Hull was killed, while Garcia managed to survive by lying still and pretending to be dead. Throughout the rest of January, Woodfield committed several more robberies and assaults as he moved towards southern Oregon, still using Interstate 5 as his main means of travel, leaving behind a trail of crimes in his wake.

Woodfield escalated to murder once more in February of 1981. This time, Woodfield would have traveled from Oregon into California, causing his crime spree to be spread over three different states. It was on February 3rd that the bodies of 37 year old Donna

Eckard and her 14 year old daughter, Jannell Jarvis, were found in their home in Mountain Gate, California. The crime was gruesome. Mother and daughter were shot multiple times in the head. It was only later revealed, after tests had been conducted on the bodies, that 14 year old Jannell had been sodomized before her death.

The rape and murders of Eckard and Jarvis were not the only crimes that Woodfield allegedly committed that day. Police discovered that earlier in the day on February 3rd, only 15 miles away in Redding, California, a female clerk in a store had been kidnapped during an armed robbery. She had also been raped and sodomized during the event. The crimes were so similar, it was clear the whoever had committed the crimes against Eckard and her daughter had also committed the rape of the young store clerk during the robbery. On February 4th, in Yreka, California, which was 100 miles away from the incidents committed the day before, a man was reported to have raped and sodomized another woman during a robbery. On the evening of the 4th, the same man robbed a motel in Ashland, Oregon.

The crime spree up and down the I-5 was becoming a nightmare. The I-5 Bandit was causing trauma and mayhem wherever he went, with hundreds of miles stretched between each incident, making it almost impossible for law enforcement to tell where he would strike next. The only thing anyone knew was that it would be along the I-5, but with 1,400 miles of ribbon stretched between Canada and Mexico, that could have been anywhere. Women were being told that they needed to be careful, but there was no place to pinpoint where and who was at risk. Woodfield did not seem to discriminate in his targets, other than that they were female: from an eight year old girl to a late-thirties woman, no female seemed to be safe if they were in the wrong place at the wrong time.

February 14th, 1981, an eighteen year old girl by the name of Julie Reitz was shot and killed inside the home of her and her mother, Candee Wilson. Julie was no stranger to Woodfield. He had once let her into a club when she didn't have a legitimate ID. Reitz would mark the third victim of the I-5 Killer that could be directly tied back to Woodfield. The murder of Julie Reitz took place in Beaverton, Oregon, miles and miles away from the last attacks in California. Woodfield was using the I-5 to terrorize everyone, everywhere, seemingly able to disappear from one town and popup in the next in the blink of an eye.

Despite evading law enforcement during the early stages of their investigation into the deaths of Cherie Ayers, Darcey Fix and Douglas Atlig, Randall Woodfield was a prime suspect by police investigators into the many crimes of the I-5 Bandit - and now, too, the I-5 Killer. Woodfield was easily connected to the crimes by police due to the fact that he was connected with several of the victims, and the victims of the crimes that were not connected to Woodfield, personally, still demonstrated the I-5 Killer's M.O. While the investigation turned to Woodfield, the I-5 killer was able to strike several more times before law enforcement were able to get a lead on him. Between February 15th and February 28th, Woodfield managed two more robberies and sexual assaults. Even after having the suspicion and full-focus of police investigators into his crimes, Woodfield was still a terror along the Interstate, wrecking havoc with no foreseeable way to stop him.

Finally, law enforcement got the help they needed. Lisa Garcia, the woman that Woodfield had accidentally left for dead during his attached on Garcia and Sheri Hull, played an instrumental part helping law enforcement finally bring Woodfield down. She worked with the lead investigator on the case, David Kominek, who worked tirelessly and who had already considered Randall Woodfield a suspect back from the Hull murder.

Garcia picked Woodfield out from a line up as the man who had come into her offer and shot and murdered in co-worker, and left her wounded and thought dead. It was this, along with paycard record showing Woodfield making calls up and down the I-5 within miles of where the crime scenes were located, that allowed police to finally make the move to bring Woodfield in for an interrogation.

On March 5th, 1981, Randall Woodfield was brought in for interrogation while police searched his home. Woodfield happened to be staying in a room he was renting from a family in Springfield, Oregon, who had no idea of what their tenant was up to. In his room, police discovered the same brand of tape that had been used to bind some of the victims, as well as a .32 bullet—the same gun used and missing from the Fix murder. The evidence mounted quickly against him, and Woodfield was charged on March 9th, 1981 with the murder of Shari Hull, the attempted murder of Lisa Garcia, and two counts of sodomy. Perhaps it is of little surprise what Woodfield, along with his public defender, plead not guilty to the charges.

From Washington to Oregon, indictments began coming in with charges like: rape, murder, sodomy, attempted kidnapping and armed robbery. In the summer of 1981, the I-5 Killer finally stood trial for all of his crimes in his hometown of Salem, Oregon. Woodfield's not guilty defense hinged on a case of mistaken identity, despite the surmounting evidence against him. The prosecutor of the case described Woodfield as "an arrogant, cold, unemotional individual". The author of the book *The I-5 Killer*, Ann Rule, who spent years covering this case, described Woodfield as "humbled". She said, "He looked, if anything, humbled—a predatory creature brought down and caged in mid-rampage." When it was Woodfield's turn to take the stand, Rule describes him a being incredibly soft spoken. He was still handsome at 30 years old, looking much like he had during his football star glory days.

While Woodfield is handsome, quiet, polite and charismatic, one thing is also clear: he holds no responsibility for his actions, and has no accountability to himself for the crimes he committed. He shows no remorse for what he's done. The evidence against him was enough to counterbalance the soft-spoken personality that Woodfield exhibited in court.

The jury came back in short time. The verdict was in. On June 26th in 1981, Randall Woodfield was found guilty on all four counts: murder, attempted murder, and two counts of sodomy. Oregon does not have the death penalty, and so Woodfield was sentenced to life in prison with an additional 90 years. Unlike Woodfield's first stint in prison, where his ten years was cut short and the would-be killer was released onto the unsuspecting victims he would later enact horrific cruelties on, this sentence was final. Woodfield would not be released again.

After his conviction, other jurisdictions up and down the Interstate 5 would have to decided whether or not they wanted to pursue charging Woodfield with additional crimes. After taking into account the state costs, and the fact that Woodfield would not live to see the end of his sentence, nor would he ever be released from prison, it was decided not to charge Woodfield with the additional counts of murder, rape and robbery that he committed while driving up and down the I-5.

Despite his conviction, and despite other jurisdictions deciding to forgo charging him with any more crimes, Woodfield's crimes continued to add up throughout the years following the trial. With the help of DNA testing, Woodfield was linked to the murders of Darcey Fix, Douglas Altig, Donna Eckard and her daughter Jannell Jarvis, and Julie Reitz. Altogether, despite having no link to the crimes, Woodfield is still suspected of up to 44 homicides with similar M.O's to the I-5 Killer's trail of crimes and victims.

At the age of 66, Woodfield is now living out the rest of his life only a mile away from Interstate 5. He serving out his life sentence and consecutive additional 90 years at the Oregon State Penitentiary in his hometown of Salem, Oregon. While imprisoned, he has been married three times, two of which had ended in divorce.

In 2005, a former police lieutenant went to visit Woodfield in prison in an attempt to garner a confession of related crimes. The lieutenant described Woodfield as charismatic, saying, "He was very charismatic, which makes sense because he would lure victims and get them to let their guard down." However, Woodfield would not confess to any crimes, and was known to stop talking whenever the subject would turn away from anything but football and sports. In 2006, Woodfield signed up for a Myspace page where he admitted to one murder and "many other crimes". Altogether, however, Woodfield does not admit to his slew of heinous crimes that had, for two long years, plagued the residences of Washington to California with fear.